The Spoken Word: A Public Speaking Handbook

The Spoken Word: A Public Speaking Handbook

First Edition

Calvin L. Troup, Ph.D.
Geneva College

Editor: Joel S. Ward, Ph.D.

Copy Editor: Erika Kauffman

Layout: Caleb McCracken

Cover Design: Lily Mann

First edition published 2021

by Geneva College

3200 College Avenue, Beaver Falls, PA 15010

Typeset in Goudy Old Style (OTF) by

Caleb McCracken, Beaver Falls, PA

Printed and Bound in the United States of America by Geneva College.

Library of Congress Control Number: 2021915634

About *The Spoken Word: A Public Speaking Handbook*

This book stands upon millennia of handbooks on rhetoric and oratory. The handbook tradition promotes practical instruction and ready reference toward mastery of the spoken word in the real world. As Aristotle notes in *The Rhetoric*, Book II, the principles engaged here apply to groups, but also when speaking with just one person. Handbooks, including *The Spoken Word*, are designed to be useful for beginning, advanced, and accomplished speakers. A good handbook invites speakers deeper and deeper into the substance of rhetoric and oratory at work.

Calvin L. Troup, Ph.D. About the Author

After graduating from Geneva College, Beaver Falls, Pennsylvania, in 1983, Calvin L. Troup, Ph.D., worked in Washington, D.C. as a trend analyst for The Naisbitt Group, a congressional staff aide to Rep. Duncan Hunter, and an association executive with the National Association of Life Underwriters.

Troup has been teaching public speaking since 1989, when he entered the graduate program in the Department of Speech Communication at The Pennsylvania State University, earning a master's degree (1991) and Ph.D. (1994). He taught public speaking at Penn State and directed the Basic Public Speaking Course at Indiana University in Bloomington, Indiana, and at Duquesne University in Pittsburgh, Pennsylvania. Troup also taught public speaking workshops for managers and supervisors at the Mon Valley Works of United States Steel for more than a decade and has been teaching the dynamics of public speaking annually at the Reformed Presbyterian Theological Seminary in Pittsburgh for more than fifteen years.

Troup's scholarly work focuses on Rhetoric and Philosophy of Communication, particularly the Rhetoric and Philosophy of St. Augustine, and on the study of Media Ecology. He has published several books and articles in addition to editing the *Journal of Communication and Religion* and serving as past president of the Religious Communication Association.

In 2016, Troup was elected by the Geneva College Board of Trustees to serve as the College's twentieth president.

Preface

To speak well in public does not require a special talent, temperament, or personality type. Ordinary people can learn the art of public speaking.

If you're working on improving your public speaking, it may be you have important ideas to share, face important issues, and need to communicate well with others to get important things done in the world. We can all extend and enhance our capacity to speak in public.

Articulate speech is both a common attribute we share and a unique dynamic that links us to one another.

Public speaking is a practical art through which you use speech to coordinate thought, work, and life between people in communities. Although it's not necessarily comfortable or easy, public speaking is something you can learn to do because you're human—you're built to speak.

You already use many of the basic skills you need for public speaking to speak well in conversation. Part of the challenge is to translate your conversational abilities into a public speaking context.

People like us have been doing this successfully for millennia. Ordinary citizens have been taking speech courses since before Aristotle's *Rhetoric* (c. 350 B.C.). In fact, in ancient times, many influential and intelligent people took speech courses, but never learned to read and write. Education focused on orality—the practices of oral communication—not literacy. When literacy levels skyrocketed following the introduction of the printing press, education shifted from oral communication to reading and writing. Therefore, people today feel more comfortable with text. Reading, writing, keyboarding, texting, viewing and listening are all more familiar and comfortable than public speaking.

But we cannot learn to speak well based on texts and images. We have to listen and speak with one another in person.

The face-to-face listening and speaking involved in public speaking classes and training exercises help us to develop the mental pathways associated with orality. Oral patterns of thought and presentation cultivate the personal presence we need to speak well in public situations. We already have the basic capacities; we were born with them. But for most of us, these capacities are now "residual" or underdeveloped.[i]

[i]Walter Ong, *Orality & Lieteracy: The Technologizing of the Word*. Orality now exists in a residual form for highly literate people.

The Spoken Word is a handbook for use as a prompt and a guide to:

1. Cultivate your innate mental capacity for presentations in public;

2. Engage audiences and hold their attention with listener-friendly oral patterns of thought;

3. Strengthen in-person public speaking skills.

Your job is to internalize the principles and practices of orality through deliberate, thoughtful practice. *The Spoken Word* provides basic forms. To learn the contours of public speaking, you will work from the basic forms to develop personal applications. In the process, you will gain new cognitive abilities and oral communication skills; you'll be better equipped to serve the people, groups, and communities with whom you live and work. You'll be able to think within the spoken word and invite others to think with you—to excel at thinking on your feet as you speak in public.

Contents

Work in the Spoken Word 1

"If a person is not behind his [or her] words, it's mere noise." ~ **Jacques Ellul**[1]

[1]Jacques Ellul. *The Humiliation of the Word*, trans. Joyce Main Hanks (Grand Rapids, MI: Eerdmanns,1985), 157.

You want to speak with eloquence. You want your message to be organized and coherent. You want to be heard and understood. You want to be able to hold people's attention. When a message is meaningful, you want people to get it.

Have you ever listened to a speaker who was able to stand up in front of a large group, look people in the eye, and talk with the audience about something that really mattered to listeners without depending on notes or reading a script?

You can learn to do this too...by learning to work in the spoken word.

Working in the spoken word means learning how to work "off script." To move from competence as a speaker toward real command of the speaking situation, you have to abandon writing techniques. You don't "write speeches," you design speeches for oral presentation from the start, using principles of the spoken word. The transition from writing-based techniques to the spoken word will transform your ability to think and speak publicly on your feet.

Most of us are pretty comfortable in informal conversation, but our oral capacities remain residual, or underdeveloped, for public speaking purposes.[2] But you can cultivate your oral capacities for public speaking purposes and learn to excel as a public speaker.

[2]Walter Ong, *Orality & Literacy. The Technologizing of the Word* (New York, NY: Routledge, 2002). Orality is now a residue for literate people.

The Spoken Word will help you learn basic oral forms to enhance public speaking, then practice them in person. The handbook works as a prompt and a guide to:

(1) Awaken and develop your innate mental capacities for public speaking (chapters 2-3),

(2) Foster oral patterns of thought to engage listeners via auditory apparatus (chapters 4-5), and

(3) Cultivate your personal presence in public speaking contexts (chapters 6-7).

Our goal is to enhance the quality of your public speaking performance in professional, communal, and personal situations.

PURPOSE: *Start working in the spoken word–public speaking in person.*

PRINCIPLE: *Build good speaking practices by stimulating your existing mental capacity for oral thought and performance.*

PRACTICE: *Impromptu speaking*

AWAKEN ORAL PATHWAYS

Ordinary people can learn the art of public speaking. You don't need a special talent, temperament, or personality type. Articulate speech is a unique dynamic that links us together as human beings. Therefore, we can all extend and enhance our capacity to speak in public.

During personal conversation, you're already doing many of the things necessary to be a fine public speaker. You relate experiences, think through issues, reason things out with people, tell stories, give examples, and make decisions. Your family, friends, and co-workers pay attention (most of the time) and are responsive when you interact with them.

Transferring these skills into a public speaking environment is challenging. Speaking in public involves additional dimensions and dynamics. For one thing, the stakes are higher. We want to deal with important issues and need to work with others to get important things done in our worlds. Speaking in public doesn't feel like a comfortable, informal conversation to us because it's not "just the same" as an informal conversation.

But the challenge of public speaking is worth the effort.

Although it's not comfortable or easy, public speaking is something you can learn to do well because you are human, and we're built to speak. There's a big payoff, too: Public speaking contributes to good group decisions and good personal decisions. Within the spoken word we collaborate; we celebrate; and we deliberate.

As you work through the material in this handbook, do the exercises, and implement your ideas and skills in actual presentations, you'll awaken native mental capacities designed for speaking well. Hopefully, you'll find good starting points here to help you work in the spoken word and flourish as a speaker.

If Speaking Is Natural for Human Beings, Why Do We Need to Learn How?

Many people think great speakers are born, not made. It may be true that a few people have special speaking talent, but most good speakers earned their skill and effectiveness through hard work, careful attention to the art of speaking, and experience.

Talking is natural, but speaking well is not.

You need to master the spoken word to communicate fully and freely...in person.

The spoken word demands listening and speaking with people and ideas in real time. No time delay, no editing a text–instant communication. To work in the spoken word means making direct eye contact under pressure, when something is at stake; maintaining full, personal presence; and practicing solid communication skills throughout. Public speaking develops a range of skills in you that is exclusive to the spoken word.

We get work done together with speech.

Healthy communities and workplaces depend upon people well acquainted with the ways of the spoken word.

Speech is a dominant feature in creative work, decision-making, and action. Public speaking is indispensable for real participation in a wide range of professions.[3] If you can't listen and speak well in person at pivotal moments, you will remain a spectator forever.

The spoken word is a lost art.

The principles and practices of the spoken word apply in many public communication contexts–formal and informal.

We're unschooled in the spoken word–listening and speaking–and it shows. In ancient times, education focused on orality: oral principles of thought, oral pathways, and oral skills. Few people

[3]For example, a recent search on ProQuest limited to business publications produced the following examples and dozens more: Tom Reid. "Scared speechless." Contract Management 1 Nov. 2007: 54-56,58; Alex Taylor III. "TEST DRIVER. " Fortune 30 Oct. 2006: 106; Sarah B Hood. "Crowd control. " Canadian Business 27 Sep. 2004: 87-90; Jacqui Harper. "Presentation skills. " Industrial and Commercial Training 36.2/3 (2004): 125-127; Barbara Wirtz. "Public speaking: An accounting marketing tool. " The National Public Accountant 1 Apr. 2003: 14-15.

were literate. Since the printing press, education has shifted almost exclusively to reading and writing. So today we're highly literate, but we're basically lost as public speakers.

We may dread public speaking because we want to become good speakers but don't know where to start. We think that speaking well should be simple, that giving a good speech should be like writing a good essay or report. But it is not.

The spoken word behaves much differently than the written word.

We need to speak well with others in person. We know that the spoken word matters in public, but we can't learn to speak well by writing essays and memorizing them or reading them aloud. We need to work within the spoken word to get fully behind our words.

What Makes the Spoken Word Distinct?

We hear the spoken word directly and internally. We can't hold it at a distance.

"Sound incorporates...sound pours into the hearer...there is no way to immerse yourself similarly in sight," says Walter J. Ong.[4] Sound is our most basic shared communication medium, but print and images give the impression that most public thought is about sight. We can decide not to look or not to read. In contrast, speech comes into our world more immediately, more personally, and more insistently.

[4]Walter J. Ong, *Orality and Literacy: The Technologizing of the Word* (New York: Routledge, 2002), 72.

We hear the spoken word as a unity of person, thought, and emotion.

Is tone-of-voice a verbal or non-verbal quality of speech? Answer by the book and you might say "non-verbal." If you play it by ear, the question does not really make sense. In the here and now, the person, the voice, the words, and the emotions function as a whole, all at once.[5]

[5]Mikhail Bakhtin, "Discourse in Life and Discourse in Art," in *Literary Criticism and Theory: The Greeks to the Present*, ed. Robert Con Davis and Laurie Fink (White Plains, NY: Longman, 1989), 594-613.

We remember the spoken word through common patterns, not complex outlines.

The spoken word resonates with others via common patterns of thought. The world of sound resists intricate organization. Therefore, good speakers introduce new ideas through basic, common sense structures. When we use complicated patterns, even smart listeners can get lost. Sophisticated ideas? Yes. Complicated structures? No.

The Spoken Word Is More Than How to Give a Speech

Training in speaking methods and techniques can make you an effective "one-trick" speaker, but it will not help you to speak well under pressure. You can learn how to give a sales pitch, how to present a report, how to talk your way through a slide presentation, or how to explain a safety procedure.

By contrast, learning public speaking as an art with a broad spectrum of skills can develop habits of thought and practice that enhance communication in every aspect of life. For instance, work in the spoken word can help you to:

Answer questions

Q&A is often a deal maker (or breaker). When the speech ends in the real world, your work is half done. Many decisions in real life turn on thoughtful responses, not prepared remarks. Learning to think on your feet in the speech can help to cultivate real time listening and speaking skills for Q&A. The importance of Q&A skills cannot be overestimated.

Lead meetings.

You need the art of public speaking to chair a meeting well. The principles and practices of the spoken word are indispensable when you are responsible to locate and define the issues, organize an agenda, and guide interaction through eye contact and non-verbal cues. For instance, good speaking skills can help you to invite insights from the quiet and temper the outspoken with grace.

Train and teach.

Good teaching includes an element of public speaking performance. Trainers, teachers, directors, and coaches excel by working through the spoken word. Instructional leadership combines basic public speaking skills, Q&A, and meeting management in interactive contexts.

LISTEN

"We have two ears and one mouth so that we can listen twice as much as we speak."
~ Epictetus[6]

"Everyone should be quick to listen, slow to speak and slow to become angry."
~ The Book of James[7]

[6]Epictetus, *The Works of Epictetus*, vol. 1-2 of *Discourses*, trans. Thomas Wentworth Higginson (Boston, MA: Little, Brown, and Company, 1912), 277.

[7]James 1:19 (Revised Standard Version).

Listen First

Our two ears function in language long before we are able to speak. We take this natural precedent as a clue for good public speaking. Not only are we called into being and consciousness through speech, we are also called upon to speak. Persons and circumstances call us. We respond with speech...and with speeches!

Since speech is a responsive act, we do well as speakers to listen with care for indicators that we might need to respond to someone about something that matters—something that needs to be dealt with now. We can listen for answers to basic questions:

Who calls us to speak?

Other persons. Whether formally or informally, directly or indirectly, in-person or remote, other persons invite, assign, require, or even incite us to speak. When we speak we're responding to the words and actions of another person or group of people. And ordinarily, someone needs us to speak with them, to them, or for them. As we have already heard, speaking is a uniquely human and personal act.

We need to make it our practice to listen for who is calling us to speak.

What calls us to speak?

Circumstances of life. We are called to speak by what is happening around us. Life is dynamic and we respond to the realities of life that press upon us—challenges and opportunities, needs and desires—through speech. As people, we are placed within situations not entirely of our own making. In this sense we always speak "on location" (for specific locations, see below).

We need to listen for what in our world is calling us to speak.

Where are we called to speak?

In person, to live audiences in the crucial, backstage, off-screen moments of ordinary human life. We are often called to speak within small and mid-sized work teams, businesses, and other firms; within communities; within non-profit organizations; within schools; within civic and political contexts; within religious communities and institutions: Where most people live and work out what matters most in all walks of life within free societies.[8] (Note: Speeches by public figures for news media outlets—whether politicians, entertainers, news commentators, or other public personalities—follow a different speaking model altogether.[9] Such speeches are mediocre and painful for listeners, even for fans and supporters who must pretend enthusiastic support.)

[8]The term comes from Gerard A. Hauser, *Vernacular Voices: The Rhetoric of Publics and Public Spheres* (University of South Carolina Press, 1999).

[9]J. Michael Sproule, "The New Managerial Rhetoric and the Old Criticism," *Quarterly Journal of Speech* 74, no. 4(1988): 468-486.

We need to listen for *where* we will meet our audience—not just a site, but the mindset(s), background(s), and current situation(s) from which the audience will be listening.

When are we called to speak?

Now, and at the appropriate time. We need to listen when we're called and listen for when we are being called to speak. We hear a call to speak in the present, and the call may persist. But often the time is ripe for a good word and you don't want to miss the moment. At the same time, the call often leads us to prepare to speak soon—at a pending event, an appointed time in the *near* future.

Reading can be taken up or put down. But speech-in-person is more compelling; it unites both speaker and listeners in a shared, present moment. In speech, timing is almost everything.

Why are we called to speak?

> *To answer well for others.* According to our various roles and responsibilities, we owe people good answers. We may reply to a specific question or answer a call to speak on an emerging problem that demands attention. In any case, speeches are part of ongoing conversations in which we are called to participate as speakers.
>
> We need to listen for the *questions, problems, and issues* that call us to speak, and we need to discern when it's within our role to speak and when it's not.

Solomon the Wise said that to answer before listening is foolish and shameful (see Proverbs 18:13). To listen first gives us a chance to assess the speaking situation and hope to provide a good answer for our audience. Listening gives us a hope that by speaking-in-person we can craft a timely response within the realm of practical wisdom.

Listen for Content

Listening well is the basis for practicing wisdom, eloquence, and virtue. If you are going to bring a meaningful message to your audience, you have to listen well for what really matters. Your charge as a speaker is not to gather information. Good speeches do not come from elaborate research methodologies or effective data collection; they require discernment. A good speech emerges from careful interpretation of content, which makes listening pivotal to good thought. Therefore,

- listen for reliable *knowledge* from trusted people;
- listen for resonant *stories* through which a good message can be advanced;
- listen for common sense *reasons* that will stimulate good thinking in your listeners; and
- listen for good *ideas*, wherever they can be found.

Listen in and through the language of others, including a wide range of thoughts, emotions, and insights. Familiarize yourself with the people you're relying on for the content of your message. The strength of your message depends on quality content—the kind you and your listeners can believe in—including late contributions that strengthen the message even as you prepare the speech.

WISDOM & ELOQUENCE IN SPEAKING

Men ought not the less to devote themselves to eloquence, although some men both in private and public affairs misuse it in a perverse manner; but I think rather that they should apply themselves to it with the more eagerness, in order to prevent wicked men from getting the greatest power to the exceeding injury of the good, and the common calamity of all men; especially as this is the only thing which is of the greatest influence on all affairs both public and private; and as it is by this same quality that life is rendered safe, and honourable, and illustrious, and pleasant. For it is from this source that the most numerous advantages accrue to the republic, if only it be accompanied by wisdom, that governor of all human affairs.

~Cicero, *On Invention*, Book I. iv

Listen to the Audience

To speak in public is to speak in person. We know that face-to-face interaction is the richest form of human communication available. But how can you listen to an audience as a speaker, especially when the audience is supposed to be sitting quietly and listening to you?

You have to *listen with your eyes!*

Many speakers can't listen with their eyes. They can't tolerate direct eye contact. What's the prime culprit? Stage fright. Inexperienced speakers need to learn how to manage stage fright well. To become good speakers, we must depend on direct eye contact not to make a good impression on listeners, but to listen to our audience.

The Reality of Stage Fright

Every speaker must learn how to deal with some degree of stage fright. We'll look at the physiology of stage fright, then discuss some basic practices through which you can move from avoiding direct eye contact to "listening" with your eyes.

[10]Comparison produced by Colleen Carron DeLong, Ph.D. Used with permission.

PHYSIOLOGY OF STAGE FRIGHT [10]

Public speaking is a common fear, even among seasoned speakers. The degree of stage fright varies depending on the perceived threat. The comparison below shows predictable speaker experiences during a "fight or flight" response. Our bodies tend to respond similarly to threatening situations.

PHYSICAL CONDITION	SPEAKER EXPERIENCE
Perceived Danger.	Fear of Speaking.
Adrenaline Rush.	Alertness/Anxiety.
Blood Circulates Faster.	Heart Rate Increases.
Glycogen Depletes Oxygen.	Out of Breath/Panting.
Glycogen to Extremities for FIGHT or FLIGHT.	Hands and Knees Shake. Nervous Twitches and Habits Appear. Shifting Feet.
Muscles Get Blood Priority. Digestion Stops!	Butterflies. Cotton Mouth.
Blood Rushes to Capillaries.	Blushing.
Excess Waste Removed from Blood.	Sweaty Palms, Etc.
Need for Oxygen Causes Involuntary Air Movement in Throat.	Words Hard to Say. Voice Cracks. Involuntary Squeaks.
Talking Counter-Productive to FIGHT or FLIGHT.	Avoid Eye Contact. Verbal Pauses. Mental Blocks.

Fight or flight.

Stage fright is natural. The anxiety most of us experience before a speech is common and healthy–it's not a phobia. In fact, if you don't feel any anticipation, you may not be human! The fear we feel when many sets of eyes are fixed on us activates a physiological reaction that results in an involuntary physical effect called a "fight or flight response." Our mind reads "danger" and our body wants to take off or take on the threat.

The table above sketches out the fight or flight response. We don't always progress through every stage. Usually we feel the most distress just before we speak and right after the speech starts. We want to shut up and run, just when we're supposed to stand still and be articulate. Thankfully, about one minute after we start speaking, the fight or flight response dissipates after which we feel more comfortable, more composed, and even more confident.

Stakes of speech.

Stage fright is predictable. Why does public speaking cause fear? Speaking is a high-stakes performance environment for us personally and professionally. We feel conspicuous and exposed with so many sets of eyes focused on us. We don't want to be embarrassed and we fear criticism. Even great speakers get nervous. But most don't feel severe anxiety because it's possible to *learn* to perform well under pressure.

Inside vs. outside.

Stage fright is manageable. What you feel inside doesn't show on the outside. Despite the discomfort, you can still excel at public speaking. You can feel like you're freaking out and still look calm, cool, and collected.

Most times, you look better than you feel. Your voice is smoother than it feels. You feel like you're shaking, but you're not. Only your close friends could tell you're nervous. But when the speech is important to you, you'll still get these feelings, even when no one else can tell. So expect stage fright; it's a common experience. Some degree of anticipation makes sense. The point is to teach your butterflies to fly in formation.

Managing Stage Fright

Because you can anticipate stage fright, you should have a plan to manage it and make the energy of anticipation work for you. In the process, you'll be learning to make and maintain direct eye contact and to be able to listen to your audience with your eyes.

Use simple organization.

Reduce anxiety with a common-sense speech structure that is easy to remember. A basic plan that you can remember, without referring to notes, makes it hard to get lost. Find a pattern that feels logical to you—where every major move is a natural progression in your mind. For instance, simple Problem-Solution, Cause-Effect, and Chronological/Step-by-Step structures follow well-worn mental paths to make recall easy. When you can talk through your speech plan from beginning to end without notes, you won't have to fear getting lost.

Design smart notes and visuals.

Good notes and visuals can eliminate the fear of forgetting what to say. Most of us worry about losing our way or just plain "blanking out." You can manage this fear by creating:

- Prompts, Not a Script. Emphasize flow; minimize detail.

  Most people prepare complicated outlines, thinking that the detail will help them manage their fear of forgetting. Extensive details and copious notes make fears worse. People tend to keep adding details that further intensify fear. "There's so much to remember, I'm sure to forget something!"

  If you lose your way in your speech, you don't need details, you need general directions. So consider creating a simple flow chart that helps you picture the speech as a whole. Design notes and visuals as basic cue cards rather than as a script that tells you exactly what to say. This will help you to keep your eyes on the audience, not your notes.

- Simple Notes. Large print, few words.

  If your notes were on a table or low stand, could you read them easily from a few feet away? Or would you have to bend over low or pick them up to read them? Struggling to locate a helpful note in tiny print is a prime way to generate more fear.

  Prepare simple notes that you can read at a glance and can trust in a crisis. *No details. No fine print. Stick to what counts.* Make your notes road signs through the speech. You know where you're going, but want reminders and a few directions along the way.

- Visualize Quotes and Facts. Make crucial information impossible to forget.

  A few facts, statements, and ideas must not be forgotten. Don't try to memorize these key items if you don't already know them inside-out. Instead, put them on visuals aids, write them out in large print in notes, or both.

  If you have pages of text on this material, you don't know what's important yet.

  But when you have a few key facts within easy reach, you can just read them or refer to them verbatim (word-for-word) at crucial points in the speech. (It's fine to read from a notecard, visual, or directly from a source at such points in the speech.)

Practice for familiarity (don't rehearse).

Work to remember familiar ideas, not specific sentences. Your goal is to present the message as a prepared conversation. Don't rehearse like an actor repeating the same lines to memorize. That will make the fear worse because you'll be training yourself to want to say the words the same way every time.

Prepare like you would for an important conversation. Some of the best practice time can be spent simply talking through a section of the speech informally with a friend or associate.

Practice differently each time you work on the message. You'll use the same key ideas and organizational structure, and some things will sound similar. But change the way you say things on purpose.

There are many good ways to say something. If you get attached to specific sentences, you'll be tempted to memorize—a special form of drudgery that also elevates fear.

Stage fright management pitfalls.

Avoid these statements of conventional foolishness.

- I can manage stage fright simply by knowing my material well. You'll review familiar material instead of preparing a good delivery plan and practicing. You'll deserve the fear you'll feel.
- I can manage stage fright by writing out my speech. You'll read your speech, minimize eye contact, and drone the audience to distraction. Your fear of failure will be justified.
- I can manage stage fright by memorizing my speech. You'll sound robotic and serve as a mere transmitter—that is, you'll be mediocre and you'll fear blanking out!
- I can manage stage fright by looking above my listeners' heads. (They'll think I'm making eye contact.) Nonsense. They can tell whether you're looking them in the eye from even a great distance.
- I can manage stage fright by imagining my audience in their underwear (or less). Imagine the audience when they're right in front of you. Learn to look them in the eye. (You'll get used to it.)[11]

[11]Julie Schlosser, "Don't picture the audience naked," *Fortune*, November 2002, 46.

To work well in the spoken word means to listen first and listen well. Listening first means we attend by ear to a call to respond within a conversation already in progress. We respond to other people, other words, and other ideas in a context where our response may contribute something that matters for listeners and prompts yet other meaningful responses.

To listen for content means that we prepare speeches as responses, and we listen and interpret knowledge, stories, and reasons—many of which we already know and some that we learn as we craft a message for the present moment.

To listen to the audience means to learn to "listen with our eyes." Therefore, we have to manage stage fright and learn to establish and maintain direct eye contact with the audience. We must use strategies to overcome fear, plan our speech, and practice within the patterns of the spoken word. By doing so, we'll be in the best position to speak-in-person and utilize the rich interaction available only in a face-to-face environment.

SPEAK TRUTHFULLY

Conversations about ethics and morality often end prematurely when someone repeats a popular skeptical line ordinarily stated in the form of a question, "According to whose ethics?" But as Sissela Bok notes, we live in a world where basic trustworthiness is essential; a world in which deceit and lies shatter lives and destroy communities.[12]

[12]Sissela Bok, *Lying: Moral Choice in Public and Private Life*, (Vintage, 1999), 18, 31. Also see Bok's more recent *Common Values*.

Bok's work suggests that perhaps we can practice public speaking ethics on the basic ethical principles of justice and peace, deep ethical norms that protect human dignity and apply to every speaker and listener.

As Bok and many others have discovered, civilizations uniformly adopt codes against violence and deceit. The codes follow patterns that suggest a few common ethical principles that apply in most cultures, times, and places. These basic values are deeply held and vigorously enforced worldwide. Public speakers need to honor and enact these principles, principles that prohibit deceit as a direct, potent threat to human social life and our common good.

TRUTH AND APPEARANCES

Speak in such a way that your words conform to justice
and seem to conform to justice.

-Giambattista Vico

Listeners judge the content of your character by the ethical quality of your public speaking. They can, they should, and they will. To challenge an audience's ethical sensibilities is simple; to recover your credibility based on such a challenge is nearly impossible.

What Makes for a Credible Speaker?

The audience controls credibility—you can only earn it, never demand it. Will listeners hear you as credible? Can you be trusted?

How do audiences assess credibility? There's an old saying, "If it looks like a duck and walks like a duck and quacks like a duck..." We can all be deceived as listeners; we know that some speakers "get away" with deceit, especially with groupies and partisans. Nevertheless, in common speaking situations with real people, not celebrities, listeners are pretty perceptive.

Think about yourself as a listener: Are you gullible? Are you naïve? Are you easy to fool? Neither are they! Are you shrewd about detecting liars, cheats, and bigots? Can you tell when someone is not trustworthy (even if you can't quite say why)? So can your audience! When you discover that you have been deceived or manipulated, how do you feel?

So how should you approach the audience? With respect; without pretense. Aim for practical truthfulness, not deceit. Here are some basic credibility questions:

Do you sound trustworthy?

> *Speak in good faith.* Give priority to the audience's good and you will establish goodwill.
>
> Good faith and perfect knowledge are worlds apart. Give your best and you will build trust, despite errors and omissions. Make your viewpoint clear; disclose your biases. Audiences know that you speak from a perspective. To pretend to be "above it all"—unbiased and objective—works against trust. Fair disclosure of legitimate bias is more likely to build trust. Earning trust doesn't mean you'll win support for ideas. But trust is deeper, broader, and worth more than any particular speech. You can build trust even when an audience disagrees.
>
> Are you speaking for their good, or serving yourself? Do you seek an advantage at others' expense?

Do you appear trustworthy?

Practice what you preach. Is what you say consistent with what you do (or what you aspire to do)?

To contradict your speech by your actions on purpose is duplicity. Whether the audience knows it or not, the message is a sham. And the fact that duplicity may "work" for a speaker does not make it legitimate. "What you see is what you get!" Explain your standpoint and motives. No one is entirely authentic all the time, but listeners appreciate our attempts to be genuine.

Deeper Questions of Practical Ethics

Ethics go deeper than what the audience can initially hear and see.

How we develop and present messages reveals our character. We feel pressure to perform and impress; we fear failure in the speech and rejection by listeners. Temptations to deceive and excuse ourselves for it are great (to get the promotion, to impress friends, to make the sale, to win the election, to protect the reputation, etc.). Therefore, practicing virtue in speaking takes courage.

The practical force of your speech depends on your faithful presentation of the message, and being true to the ideas of the work of others, facts, documents, and other supporting evidence. Walter R. Fisher offers a good approach to communication ethics—narrative ethics—that can be applied to public speaking through the relationship between coherence and fidelity.[13]

[13]Walter R. Fisher, *Human Communication as Narration: Toward a Philosophy of Reason, Value and Action* (University of South Carolina Press, 1989).

Coherence: Internal Consistency.

Audiences expect a good message to be internally consistent, with form and content working together. If coherence breaks down, audiences wonder about deceit. A good speech that challenges the audience may still earn respect because coherent messages ring true. Truth and integrity of speech are synonymous in practice.

Fidelity: Resonance between Message and Experience.

Audiences expect the message to withstand scrutiny in the real world. When they examine your speech—ideas, sources, stories, etc.—does it check out? Fidelity includes how you represent others and their intentions, the reliability of your supporting material, and the accuracy of your evidence, historical accounts, anecdotes, and analyses (see "Rhetorical Tokens" below). Fidelity also involves fair, accurate disclosure of your own assumptions and standpoint.

Break faith with an audience on either front, and you risk being discredited by listeners. Remember that a speaker can break faith in a number of ways, including misrepresentation or secrecy. When there's a lot at stake, listeners discount those who disregard the truth or harm the community ...as they should.

TRUTH AND PROBABILITIES IN SPEAKING

The true and the approximately true are apprehended by the same faculty; it may also be noted that men have a sufficient natural instinct for what is true, and usually do arrive at the truth.

-Aristotle, *Rhetoric*, Book I

Truthfulness in Public Speaking

The constructive practice of truthfulness.

The challenge of public speaking ethics involves speaking truth constructively.

When we think of codes of ethics, we tend to think of dos and don'ts, especially the don'ts. But ethical public speaking is still public speaking–something we do. What are some coordinates to help us do public speaking ethically, to build up and not to tear down?

- Practice Cultural Generosity. *Extend hospitality and grace to the audience.*

  Speak with the idea that your role is to lead the audience as a "host"–serving the audience. Try to make the speech familiar to them; go to the audience and welcome them rather than expecting listeners to come to you. Good speaking has a tendency to bring people together and unite them around the common themes of a message. By honoring the cultures of listeners, you create opportunities for intercultural intersections and collaboration—whether the cultures are intramural, organizational, or international.

- Attend to Audience Needs. *Keep your focus on why listeners need the speech.*

  If you are speaking, the audience needs to hear the message. You already have it. So set your mind to work on meeting audience needs. What's the message they need to hear most? How would a person get it across to them? Of course, no living person can keep the personal implications of an important speech out of mind entirely. The issue is your focus of attention. If you focus on yourself, you'll intensify stage fright and invite greater temptation for ethical compromise.

The complex practice of truthfulness.

Ethical public speaking is more than mere accuracy. Sometimes when people speak of practical truth, they think only of honesty and equate it with accuracy. Truthfulness is much more complex. Messages should be accurate, but accuracy is not enough. Audiences don't use simplistic ethical schemes; they judge trustworthiness much more intuitively. When a speaker violates their ethical sensibilities, accuracy claims don't hold up.

The challenging practice of truthfulness.

Truthful messages are not always pleasant.

Speaking truthfully and appropriately is difficult. Part of the challenge is that truthfulness does not necessarily equal full disclosure about everything. Saying everything we think or know to everyone in every context without restraint is not truthful, honest, or ethical. Unrestrained disclosure often violates legitimate trust, injures others deeply, and compromises the common good.

- Avoid Niceness. *Direct deliberate acts of goodness to the audience—speak a good word.*

  Niceness leads to deceit. As the lead character in the movie *Hitch* says about not getting an immediate "yes" for a first date, "Of course she's going to lie to you. She's a nice person.

She doesn't want to hurt your feelings. What else is she going to do?" If you're afraid to hurt someone's feelings or delicate sensibilities, niceness tempts you to lie or use some other form of deceit.

- Speak with Courage. *When it's your purpose to offend, engage the audience boldly.*

  Good speeches often include unpopular ideas or statements that might make people uncomfortable. You have an obligation to deal carefully with hard issues and difficult questions. Make a good case for your message in a good way. Public speaking is not a therapy session; a person can take offense wrongly. A true message may find a crooked listener. Truthfulness demands tenacity. Don't lose your nerve.

- Use Rhetorical Tokens. *When you have to limit remarks due to time or discretion, include distinct markers that point to deeper support.*

  How do good speakers deal with the fact that you can't fully develop your own message, let alone present all sides of a case with limited time? Rhetorical tokens. A rhetorical token stands for something that's too big or too complex to fit into the speech–a brief statement, illustration, or example of more detailed material.[14]

  How can rhetorical tokens be used ethically? A rhetorical token is ethical if it can be fully "redeemed." That is, if the audience asks for greater depth or more backing, the speaker can deliver the details to the audience's satisfaction.

[14]The idea of rhetorical tokens is explained in greater detail in Leon H. Mayhew, *The New Public: Professional Communication and the Means of Social Influence* (Cambridge University Press, 1997).

THE COMPLEXITY OF TRUTHFULNESS: FIVE TESTS

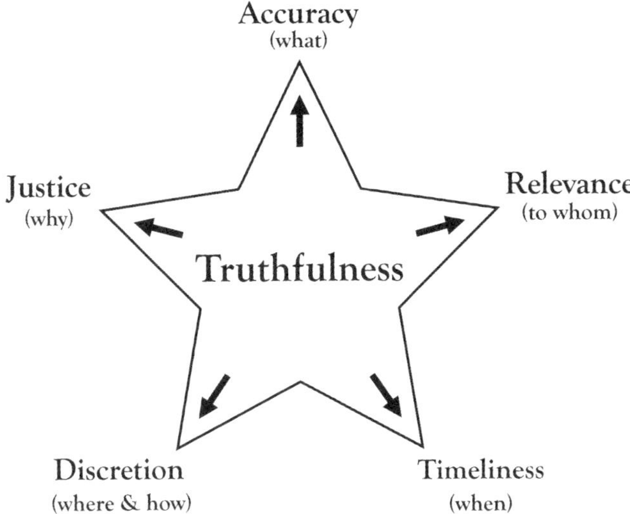

These tests provide a starting point for thinking about the complexity of truthfulness.[15] By comparison, it's easier in practice to lie or choose some other form of deceit.

[15]Five Tests adapted from Philip G. Clampitt, *Communicating for Managerial Effectivness* (Sage, 2004).

ACCURACY: WHAT? Is the message correct?

A speech could violate this test by misrepresenting statistics, falsifying quotes, tampering with documents or historical records, or plagiarism.

RELEVANCE: WHO? Should the message be presented to this audience?

A speech could violate this test by disclosing personal or professional matters that should remain private, or by disclosing a message to an audience who should not be privy to it.

TIMELINESS: WHEN? Should the message be presented now?

A speech could violate this test by premature or delayed presentation. Untimely disclosure can be disastrous.

DISCRETION: WHERE AND HOW? Should the message be presented here? In this manner?

A speech could violate this test by making a message secret that should be presented publicly, or vice-versa.

JUSTICE: WHY? What are the motives for the message?

A speech could violate this test by telling the truth to harm a person, organization, or country.

*The list is not exhaustive. It simply points to the harmony of virtues necessary for practical communication ethics in public speaking.

Ethical Pitfalls

Excellence in public speaking can lead to prominence. The lure to be self-serving entices eloquent speakers to abandon honest work and to slave for lucrative alternatives, such as personal power, affluence, and pleasure. The ethical pitfalls noted can emerge individually or in combination.

Approval.

> *The desire to be accepted and to win the favor of the audience presents ethical challenges to speakers.* Public approval won via speaking can be intoxicating.
>
> Excellent speakers receive immediate gratification from appreciative audiences; people grant them an elevated level of respect. Public recognition and personal praise make us reluctant to present unpopular messages, to speak up for those who can't speak for themselves, or to speak on controversial issues—even ones we care about deeply.

Appearances.

> *An audience's dependence on appearances presents an ethical pitfall for skilled speakers.* Eloquence can succeed using sophisticated deceits.
>
> No audience can know the heart, mind, and soul of a speaker; skill can cloak inauthenticity and mask motives, at least in the short term. What a con man can do interpersonally, an effective speaker can do en masse.

Power.

> *Through the force of eloquence, a skillful speaker can exercise unethical influence.* An effective presentation can inhabit an audience's memory in unique ways. Power is further accentuated in an era when good speaking is rare and critical thinking skills are weak.

A Note on Oral Plagiarism

To plagiarize is to claim someone else's work as your own. To plagiarize in a speech means using a whole speech, part of speech, or any other form of idea—spoken, written, etc.—from another person's work without telling the audience.

You have to tell listeners when you are relying on other people's work. When you don't say where you got the ideas, you are claiming the ideas as your own.

Being under pressure may explain the act, but it does not excuse you. People lose their jobs and students fail courses and can be dismissed for plagiarism. It doesn't always happen, but the penalty is just. Violating public trust warps the person and can deface the community.

It's fine to use someone else's work to support your speech. In fact, you're supposed to do it. Just give the person credit—tell the audience when you're relying on someone else's ideas.

IMPROMPTU SPEAKING EXERCISES

(Impromptu means "without preparation; on the spur of the moment.")

Basic format.

In this set of exercises, speakers will select or be assigned random topics. Speakers will then have a limited amount of time (usually a minute or two) to plan how to launch their message and then speak for a fixed amount of time (usually equal to the prep time).

The first speaker leaves the room with a topic for the prescribed time and prepares. When the prep time expires, the second speaker gets a topic and leaves the room and prepares while the first speaker is presenting. The pattern continues until the whole group has had an opportunity to present.

Purpose.

To stimulate oral patterns of thought for presentation, and to strengthen basic oral delivery skills–particularly direct eye contact and conversational patterns of face-to-face interaction with listeners.

Impromptu exercises help us to think on our feet about commonplace topics that we have not had time to prepare. As we learn to work as speakers with less familiar material and minimal practice, we quickly learn that we can transfer both the thought patterns and conversational delivery skills to more carefully prepared presentation.

Impromptu speaking demands mental and physical improvisation that is essential to navigating real oral presentations, particularly of longer duration, by relying on oral patterns of preparation and presentation (rather than memorization, manuscript, or extensive outlines that follow literate models of composition).

Activities.

The three impromptu speech exercises suggested below can be used as starting points from which to develop a wide array of possible impromptu exercises. All three could be used for one, two, or three minute impromptu speech exercises.

1. The Problem(s) with...are...! I propose...as a solution. Provide cards with a commonplace problem on each one (e.g., airline security; cell phones; reality TV; diets; etc.).

2. If you have to...I advise you to... Provide cards with a brief, open-ended scenario on each one (e.g., If you had to compete in the Olympic Games, I advise that you go as a...; If you had to join the military, I recommend that you serve in the...; If you had to open your own business, I'd advise that you launch a...; etc.)

3. Interpret this! Provide cards with a cliché, a maxim, a proverb, or another brief statement for each speaker to interpret for the audience.

Impromptu exercises are common. For example, Toastmasters International clubs routinely include impromptu exercises called "Table Topics" in their weekly meetings. A "Table Topics Master" is responsible to bring creative impromptu topics so that all members who are not scheduled for a formal presentation still get to speak. These activities extend the tradition that so many good speakers have found helpful and formative over many, many years.

Thinking on Your Feet 2

Get People into Action: Begining with Oral Patterns

We speak best *on our feet* about what we know best on our feet. There is actually more to it than that: We speak best *in person* about things we *know personally* that *people* have done, that *people* are doing, or that *people* need to do.

To meet audiences, locate your message in the human world of spoken words and deeds. Listeners need to hear about human decisions and actions–whether past, present, or future; real or imagined. Human choices, actions, and responses dominate good speech. The world of the spoken word is populated, located, and dynamic.

Oral patterns of thought rely on people-in-action.

In other words, the plot thickens. Work in the spoken word involves listeners in plots dedicated to human action. Audiences ask many common questions of speakers, including: *What's the story?*; *What's the point?*; and *So what?* A simple translation of the *What's the story?* question might be: *Who is involved and what did they do? /...what are they doing? /... what are they going to do?*

If you want to speak well about things that matter to listeners, you will need to focus on human problems, human decisions, and human actions. You need to keep this connection from start to finish. Speaking with oral patterns makes a message more memorable for listeners and speakers. That is why the same principles that make a good story and the practices of good storytelling are essential to excellent public speaking.

PURPOSE: *To learn how and why people-in-action make speeches meaningful and memorable.*

PRINCIPLE: *We can become dynamic speakers by placing human action at the center of the speech.*

PRACTICE: *Story exercises.*

BASIC ORAL PATTERNS

Speech is personal. The spoken word originates in a person, or persons, and is addressed directly to others in language. Information alone is of no value because it won't register with listeners.

If oral patterns of thought feature people-in-action, we need to ask: "What are the people involved in this message doing, thinking, and saying?" As speakers, we need to focus on the form and content of language that coincides with oral patterns of thought and expression. We should begin by asking basic questions: *What happened? Where? How? Who is doing what? Why? Who said so? To whom? When? What should we do about it?*

Speak for the Ear; Don't Read

How will the speech sound to the audience? Audiences use their listening apparatus when you speak.

Listening and speaking are distinct from reading and writing. Listening uses a different mental apparatus—the auditory system—and spoken language patterns are unique. Does it sound like you are reading a written report out loud, or does it sound like you are having a meaningful conversation with listeners? If you speak like you write, you'll drone. Listeners will tune you out.

Remember, you are speaking, not writing!

To speak well, you need to tune your language for the auditory apparatus of listeners. Good public speaking demands a very different use of language. Yet speakers in highly literate cultures (everywhere that text flourishes) rely on their default patterns of thought, which are dominated by written and printed texts. They prepare as though they were writing a composition—a deadly formula for speaking to living human beings.

Speaking for the ear means deliberately addressing the audience using ordinary conversational patterns. Listening and speaking demand a different approach than reading and writing. Oral patterns address:

Heart.

Listening and speaking integrate thought and emotion. People get a feel for what you are saying. Speech comes from a living person, with attitude built in through tone of voice and body language in an immediate context. Speech can only be received physically, literally within another living person. We experience speech and listening as a whole person, with reason and emotion responding together.

Mind.

Listening and speaking involve distinct mental apparatus. We use different parts of our brain to read and write than we do to speak and listen. Unless you have extensive performance training, when you read aloud or from memorization, you sound much different—usually much worse to listeners—than you do in ordinary conversation.

Action.

Listening and speaking get work done in the real world. Humans use speech to coordinate group action, and people speak internally before taking personal action. By contrast, writing emerged first and foremost as a recording device, particularly well-suited to accounting for data and details.

Oral Memory Is Different

What kind of memory do we use for thinking on our feet? Oral memory. When people think of memory and public speaking, they usually think memorization...rote memorization. Rote memorization is memory of the written word. Memory for the spoken word is about remembering ideas, patterns, key phrases, and a few crucial informational points—not sentences, paragraphs, or any other specific written structure.

The goal of oral memory is for the audience to remember the message by listening, and for the speaker to remember the speech with clarity and confidence. Oral memory allows us to think on our feet, according to a plan. We learn memory without memorization, practice without rehearsal—no drumming of words into our heads. Our goal is premeditated speaking, not recitation.

ORAL MEMORY: THINK MEMORABLE THOUGHTS

[Without writing...] How could you ever call back to mind what you had so laboriously worked out? The only answer: Think memorable thoughts. In a primary oral culture, to solve effectively the problem of retaining and retrieving carefully articulated thought, you have to do your thinking in mnemonic patterns, shaped for ready oral recurrence. Your thought must come into being in heavily rhythmic, balanced patterns, in repetitions or antithesis, in alliterations or assonances, in epithetic and other formulary expressions, in standard thematic settings (the assembly, the meal, the duel, the hero's helper, and so on), in proverbs that are constantly heard by everyone so that they come to mind readily and which they themselves are patterned for retention and ready recall, or in other mnemonic form. Serious thought is intertwined with memory systems.[1]

In an oral culture, to think through something in nonformulaic, non-patterned, non-mnemonic terms, even if it were possible, would be a waste of time.[2]

~Walter J. Ong, *Orality and Literacy*

[1]Walter Ong, *Orality & Literacy: The Technologizing of the Word* (New York, NY: Routledge, 2002), 34.

[2]Ibid., 35.

Speaking in Oral Patterns: Some Psychodynamics of Orality

Good speakers use language to help people participate in the message as listeners, not readers. In his groundbreaking book, *Orality and Literacy*, Walter J. Ong explains the major differences between the *spoken word* and the *written word.*

What's Ong's point?

Listening and speaking rely on unique mental processes that are different than reading and writing. In highly literate societies, the written word even affects the way we speak. But speakers who want to communicate well with listeners need to recognize that audiences respond better to basic oral patterns.

What does it mean to "speak in oral patterns"? The following recommendations are adapted from "Some Psychodynamics of Orality" in *Orality and Literacy.*

1. Say it simply.

Forget the formal rules of written grammar; make it sound good for listeners.

What sounds good? Conversational patterns of speech. Say it like you would say it if you were talking (because you are!). You can do things with your voice that no text can match, especially changes in vocal dynamics: tone, pace, volume, and rhythm.

Use contractions: it's, we're, don't, etc. Use clichés. Be colloquial. Use familiar language and follow familiar speech patterns–things you say but that you should not write, like "no way!" Don't worry about run-on sentences as long as you stay on track. Don't get lost: avoid rabbit trails, red herrings, and going "'round Robin's barn."

Are there any standards for spoken grammar? Yes–common spoken usage adjusted appropriately for the audience. Rules of written grammar, such as those found in Strunk & White's *Elements of Style*, don't apply to speech. Proper spoken language means "make sense!" And remember, foul language is not strong language. In speech, don't swear. Don't curse. Don't use profanity. Some accomplished speakers may choose to swear in a speech deliberately; good speakers do so rarely. No one but a fool of a speaker ever needs to resort to obscenity or profanity.[3]

[3]Charles Murray. *The Curmudgeon's Guide to Getting Ahead: Dos and Don'ts of Right Behavior, Tough Thinking, Clear Writing, and Living a Good Life* (New York: Crown Business, 2014) 27-30.

2. Apply oral labels.

Tag key people and ideas with "memory markers" throughout the speech.

Highlight priorities in the spoken word with adjectives that create labels. Nicknames and tag lines signal to listeners about how crucial players and points fit into the message.

With people, we think differently of "Honest Abe" than just Abe, "Bloody Mary" carries more freight than Mary, and "The award-winning...(person, band, team, company, etc.)"provides listeners with an oral framework. We add labels to set expectations and sharpen identification for listeners. It's not just tigers, but "the fighting tigers" or "man-eating tigers;" not just the Mississippi River, but "the mighty Mississippi" or "Old Man River;" not just a revolution, but "the glorious revolution" or "the bloody revolution;" not just a storm, but "the perfect storm" or "Super Storm Sandy."

3. Cycle back.

Return to what has been said using synonymous language.

Give listeners redundancy (on crucial points) with the spoken word. Key ideas should echo through the introduction, the specific discussion, the transitions, and into the conclusion. Simple repetition will work in some cases; creative redundancy is necessary in every case.

Traditional speech organization says, "Tell 'em what you are gonna tell 'em; Tell 'em; Tell 'em what you told 'em." This is good advice. To really make this conventional wisdom work—to cycle back—means to use oral patterns in how you do the telling.

In a speech about job interviews on the theme "connect to the work," we begin with a story from *Pursuit of Happiness*, a movie inspired by the true story of how Chris Gardner moved from homelessness in San Francisco to forge a successful career as a Wall Street stock broker. The scene shows Gardner breaking almost every formal rule of entry-level interviewing and still winning a highly selective internship position. The scene makes the point that a quality interview connects an employer's needs with a job prospect's inclination—qualification, experience, education, availability, and desire—to do the work that meets those needs. "Dress for success" is not pivotal; "connect to the work" is. To cycle back means to hit the "connect to the work" theme by including the *Pursuit of Happiness* scene in the introduction, to reinforce it at multiple transition points, and to drive it home with reference to the interview scene again in the conclusion of the speech.

4. Begin with what everybody knows.

Rely on established principles, priorities, and patterns.

Invite listeners into new ideas and situations by respecting established traditions. Proposals for the most radical changes depend most heavily on existing coordinates to gain a hearing.

Starting with what everybody knows can take different forms. A most common form is analogy. Analogical reasoning uses the familiar to help us understand the unfamiliar.

One way to find analogies that will work for listeners is to ask, "What's it like?" That is, to what in the world of the audience is the point we're trying to make similar? Good answers to these basic questions can lead us to "what everybody knows."

5. Keep it close to home.

Speak in the context of lived human experience.

To resonate with listeners, focus on concrete actions and familiar relations to people, places, and things. The spoken word works well to connect people personally and directly in time and space.

In simple terms, speak in specifics—as specific as the spectrum of the audience will allow. Talk about the Walgreens on the corner, or the CVS on Front Street, not just "a drug store." Have listeners wait at the DMV (Department of Motor Vehicles), not in a generic government office. Instead of a nameless high school teacher, let listeners struggle with a short man students nicknamed "Zippy", who has a Hitler moustache and annoyingly repeats "and so we find..." 30 times a period in your high school physics class. Generics dull our senses; specifics invite us into the message as listeners, and prompt us to make our own adjustments and translations as the speech goes on.

6. Highlight tensions.

Accent the human struggles within the message.

Call attention to the real drama—no hype. What's really at stake? Even the ordinary challenges, aspirations, and events of life get a grip on us because the spoken word engages the human condition so effectively.

How can I explain what an "entitlement mentality" means when applied to affluent kids? The tension of a typical dramatic moment in a college classroom helps:

> A college student gets a homework assignment back with a "B." She's irate. She starts complaining to the teaching assistant (TA) that "She's an "A" student!" The TA shows her the grading standards and explains patiently. But the princess just rolls her eyes and says, "Well, I guess I'll let it go this time!"

> The professor, listening with one ear, almost leaps across the two rows that separate him from the princess. "Excuse me!" he says, "The grade is correct. In fact, it is gracious—you didn't complete the work." The student demurs. "But let me be clear," continues the professor, "no one took any points away from you. From the beginning of the semester, all the points in this course are mine. You haven't lost any points. All points in this class are earned. Do you understand?" "Yes," she says. "Thank you," says the professor. And they leave the classroom.

Radio announcers who cover sporting events live and die by the spoken word. They focus on the drama of sporting events. The really good announcers heighten the drama by weaving in stories and background knowledge of the game, competitors, coaches, and teams. In many cases, sports broadcasters work in teams to add an element of dialogue by interacting with their broadcast partner(s) throughout the event.

Also note that live radio announcers, whether in news, sports, or talk formats, faithfully practice the "psychodynamics of orality". They have nicknames for players, a stock of phrases for routine plays and other occurrences, pet phrases and maxims, etc.

7. Speak to the collective heart.

Address listeners as participants, not as spectators.

Speak with listeners, do not just talk at them! The spoken word tends to link audience, speaker, and message in a community. Good speakers identify with listeners. More than a technique, this mindset links listeners and speakers, and they communicate together.

The speech is about us—not the individual speaker's self or the individual listener's self. The people involved in the message are the present company. We may not all have the same role, but we all have some meaningful stake in the action of the message.

For example, a speech for high school juniors and their parents about funding a college education should focus on the question "How are we going to afford to pay for a college education in today's world?" rather than, "What financial problems are affecting funding in higher education today?" The first question invites us into a conversation about a personal reality that most listeners are facing. The second question treats the problem at a distance, as though it may or may not apply to listeners.

8. Work in the here and now.

Concentrate on the present.

Speech drives speakers and listeners together in the *now*. All human decision-making and action occur in the *now*. The past and future are valuable when they touch on *now*. Even the decision to defer a decision is a *present* action. In speech, what was and what might be do not matter much unless they directly affect today.

We need currency to interact orally. This means relying on words, ideas, examples, and illustrations that resonate immediately with listeners. As speakers we cannot afford to define or redefine many terms.

In the world of oral communication, listeners can receive messages that go beyond what they already know. But listeners must begin, and will work best, from what's present—things we have in mind or can quickly bring to mind for present thought and action during a speech.

9. Answer the "so what?" question.

Get to the point. Make concrete applications.

Audiences are always asking, "How does this message apply to me?" and "How am I supposed to respond?" These aren't selfish questions; listeners want to know what's at stake in a message. We assume that if someone is speaking to us, there must be a practical purpose involving them. If the message does not matter to how listeners live their lives now, they won't be interested. As speakers, it is our job to make the connections.

Oral patterns help listeners make connections. Why? Because oral patterns naturally integrate knowledge, action, and experience. The spoken word reaches people right where they are.

Therefore, we need to get to the point. Get to the point early and get to the point often. At the very least, get the point on the table! If you are speaking to them then they expect to hear implications and applications for them. Hit the "so what?" questions hard or expect listeners to tune out. What listeners need aren't simple answers. Sometimes, they need concrete, compelling questions: What's the right thing to do? What should we do now? What should we do next?" Take care to answer the basic "so what?" questions directly in every speech, and rely on oral patterns to reinforce what's at stake for listeners.

Making Messages Memorable

To make an oral message memorable for an audience, it first has to be memorable for you.

IF YOU CAN'T REMEMBER WHAT YOU ARE GOING TO SAY,

(THE BASIC MESSAGE)

HOW WILL THE AUDIENCE EVER REMEMBER IT!?!

What can you do to remember your speech, especially without depending on extensive notes, a detailed outline, or a manuscript? Cultivate a good oral memory!

Start with listeners.

What helps an audience remember? Devise good memory patterns for listeners and you will remember the speech with ease. Remember that listeners do not have notes.[4] Consider that as listeners we never remember a whole speech—that's not the point. However, we can reconstruct the basic message later if the speaker gives us enough good material in a memorable way.

[4]Good speaking notes are recommended. For specific directions on design and use of notes in memorable speeches, see chapter 5 and chapter 28.

Remember without memorizing.

Expect to remember the speech. You know how to remember and do it well already. In everyday conversation, your responses aren't scripted or recited from memorized statements. Even in challenging situations, you usually remember crucial things you want to say, and you usually say them coherently.

You practice *premeditated speaking.* For instance, in a job interview, you don't know exactly how the question will be phrased, but you think through basic questions in advance:

What are my strengths? When have I overcome a challenge in a work situation? What's a real mistake I've made and how did I fix it? You prepare for what to say without memorizing, but the preparation helps you remember.

You can put this everyday skill to use for public speaking.

Create a memory game plan.

Plot your moves with mnemonic markers to guide you and your audience through the speech. A speech is more than just a casual conversation and lasts longer, so you need a game plan. A good game plan should be in your head; notes will serve only as props for practice and prompts for performance.

Oral memory patterns help you to develop existing memory skills to speak well and to enhance the audience's memory after the speech.

Cut Through the Infoglut

Audiences do not remember details, they discriminate. Listeners do not care about, nor will they remember, the details of your message. A good listening audience will only remember about 50% of what you say right after your speech is over. A week later, they will remember about 5%. Most of the details you are so worried about won't even make it out of the room with them.

Frame the speech to control which 5% the audience remembers. What will they remember? The audience is listening for themes and ideas that interest them. They will remember crucial supporting information tied to those interests. So work to make your main point unforgettable. Tie the supporting material tightly to the big ideas and main themes in the message, and cut peripheral information, digressions and tangents ruthlessly. Keep details to a minimum.

How Do You Remember Your speech?

Don't try to remember the whole thing!

You never have to remember the speech all at once. Work to remember how to move through the speech.

Remember the next speaking point.

Make the speaking point simple to remember and the whole point will be yours.

Your speaking structure should already play to memory. Use mnemonics to label each point for the ear and the mind.

Use the power of association.

Link the contents of each speaking point to physical places that are present when you speak.

For example, the venue: Label the left wall with your first speaking point and ideas. Place ideas from your second speaking point on the back wall. Use the right wall to locate ideas from the third speaking point. Put transitions between the points in the corners between each wall. (Note that you would be moving in a clockwise or typical left-to-right direction.)

Another example: your body.

Good relationships begin with distance.

Remember speaking points by associating them with the speaker's body.

1. FEET: *Walk* away from pseudo-familiarity. (Problem)
2. HANDS: *Work* from a safe distance. (Solution)
3. EYES: *Watch* for real signs of trust to grow. (Implication)

This example of building a memory has the advantage of moving in a direction from feet to head.

MEMORY IN A BUILDING

Think of a large building, Quintilian said, and walk through its numerous rooms remembering all the ornaments and furnishings in your imagination. Then give each idea to be remembered an image, and as you go through the building again deposit each image in this order in your imagination. For example, if you mentally deposit a spear in the living room, an anchor in the dining room, you will later recall that you are to speak first of war, then of the navy, etc.[5]

This system still works.

–Daniel Boorstin, *The Discoverers*

[5]Daniel J. Boorstin, *The Discoverers* (New York: Random House, INC, 1983), 481.

Oral Pattern Pitfalls

Melodrama.

Find the drama, don't force it! The drama is in the human action. Who is involved? Who is affected? Where is the tension for people? Working within the drama of the speech engages listeners. Listeners will recognize false drama, overstatement, and hype, and they will likely tune out.

Process comments.

No setup necessary. Never say, "I would like to tell you a story about..." or "Listen to how this conversation went..." or "Think about this interesting hypothetical scenario with me..." Just tell the story, include the dialogue, and proceed with the message. Oral patterns have all kinds of built-in cues that listeners recognize. Setup lines waste time and dampen attention.

Losing the point.

Keep oral patterns on message. Oral patterns are so important to good public speaking because they're much more interesting and fun for speakers and listeners than the predictable droning of written patterns. But the pluses can work against a speaker who begins to sound gimmicky and whose oral patterns are disconnected from the point of the speech. Therefore, scrap anything that does not deliberately and directly advance the message.

DIALOGUE

Put dialogue into your speech and you can let the audience listen in on real conversations. You don't need to be a great conversationalist; just aim to use your voice the way you do in everyday, ordinary conversation with people. Also, bringing the voices of other people into the message can strengthen content. Therefore, including spoken dialogue in a speech accomplishes a number of good things:

Invitation to participate.

Dialogue includes listeners in conversation. We're immediately attracted to other voices in the speech. We like to listen to what people are actually saying. We want to be involved. Incorporating dialogue involves listeners as conversational participants quite differently than explanations and descriptions in the message.

Conversations in progress.

People are already talking about what matters to them. Because a good message is well-connected to the life experience of listeners, dialogue can tune into relevant conversations already under way. Don't fool yourself into thinking you are going to communicate with people about something that is completely alien to them.

Alternatives and provocations.

Other voices help you faithfully incorporate other perspectives. Dialogue can help you put challenging ideas, audience questions, and objections on the table more credibly. Once expressed, you can consider such issues thoughtfully with listeners.

Vocal dynamics.

Speakers come to life–through dialogue their voices become more animated. By learning how to perform the voices of others, you can learn to use your own voice more conversationally–less monotonously–in a speech.

Memorability.

Listeners remember the content of the message better. The lines people remember from movies, television episodes, etc., tend to be embedded in dialogue. Why? Because the cadences and patterns of the spoken word make them memorable. Rehearsal of information does no such thing; it promotes droning in speakers and forgetfulness in listeners.

How to Work Dialogue into the Speech

Include dialogue—the voice of other people speaking—in the message (rather than talking about what they say). Build realistic speaking exchanges as you plan the speech.

What did the person/people say?

You repeat what someone has said. You may give a single statement or an account of a longer conversation. The account may be of what one person said or of a conversation among a number of people.

A favorite professor in our internship program sent us off to our assignments on the first day, saying: "The first month you'll be in the way! The second month you'll learn to get out of the way. And the third month, you'll finally feel like you're starting to make a contribution. You'll be fine. Now go and have a great day!"

How did the conversation go?

You give an account of a conversation you had. The conversation may be with a person or a group. In this case, you may present many voices involved in the conversation.

Speaking Point (Solution): Write down your questions in advance, so you won't forget. Doctors are busy people always working under pressure. Good ones have a lot of patients. So write 'em down...

I learned this from Dr. R, who would come into my hospital room at 5 a.m. after doing surgery all night. He was always chipper, with a parade of residents. I was heavily sedated and usually had been asleep for a few hours.

Dialogue: "Good Morning! How ya' feelin'?" he would say almost gleefully. "Do you mind if my students take a look at you?" (I was an interesting case.)

"Nope. Go right ahead. It's the right eye." (This was my stall tactic to reach for my notepad so I could grill Dr. R.)

"What about this?" I'd ask.

"I don't know, I only know orthopedics, but I'll talk to Dr. D. for you?"

"OK. How long until I can go home?"

"Maybe a week. But I don't send anyone home on narcotics, so you can't leave until you're on Tylenol."

"OK. See you tomorrow morning."

Return to Point: If you want to get good care, you have to have your questions prepared in advance and get those questions asked!

What might they say?

You project what a person well-known to you might say related to the message. When you're familiar and know a person well, you can dramatize what they might say in a typical conversation. If you do this, let the audience know: "I'd expect him/her to say..."

Crafting Dialogues

Construct the speech with input and interchanges from others. Treat the people speaking as characters in a play or a novel, adding their voices, attitudes, and perspectives into the speech. Be faithful to who they are and how they speak.

Plan to speak, never write.

Prepare a game plan for dialogue. Note what dialogue to include and its placement in the speech. Use quotations and dialogues that you can remember without memorizing. Don't aim for written accuracy. Listeners need faithful oral memory to engage the message because of it superiority at approximating tone and vocal animation. Spoken dialogue preserves much more meaning than the most precise text or manuscript.

Use the healthy voices in your head.

Practice partial impressions. Most of us mimic other people's voices from time to time privately. You may surprise yourself! Represent the people speaking approximately—as accurately as you can without taking lessons. Take on some aspects of the speaker's persona. Think through a primary non-verbal feature of their speaking (e.g., facial expression, posture, or gesture) that you can include in how you represent them conversationally.

Capture information.

Match conversational inflection. Review and practice how the dialogue should sound, such as the patterns of timing and tone of another person speaking.

For example:

Speaking Point: The network you need to get your next job is not your personal network, it's the network of your professional friends, neighbors, and other acquaintances.

Voice in my head to use:

Joe's boss in *Joe Versus the Volcano*, who is talking about a job applicant and saying, over and over and over again:

"I know he can DO the jawb (job), but does he WANT the jawb (job)?"

And then, in sequence, "I'm not arguing that with you!" "I'm not arguing that with you!"

Application: The decision makers are networked. They're not in the applicant's network.

Why Dialogue? Help Listeners Think Alongside the Message

You cannot speak fast enough to hold the audience's attention.

People speak at an average rate of 100-150 words per minute. But people can hear and understand speech at a rate of up to 400-600 words per minute. No wonder we can get bored so quickly in meetings!

So, how does any speaker have a chance of really engaging an audience and getting a message across? The vocal animation that comes with dialogue, especially as part of a larger story that fits the message and helps listeners get involved.

We don't need people to hang on our every word. No. We just want people to think with us about the message. When we engage an audience's imagination, they don't suddenly hear every word, think the same thing, or even get precisely the same message.

Instead, dialogue provides dynamic, dramatic words that help capture imaginations so listeners can "think alongside" the message.

Dialogue Pitfalls:

It is a speech, not a play.

Don't be melodramatic. Dialogue can be overdone in a number of ways. As one way to enhance memory, dialogue should be included with some restraint. When used discreetly, dialogue can be powerful. Overuse will kill its potential to enhance the message.

Ridicule.

Don't bring voices of others into the speech to demean them. Appropriate criticism should be spoken in your own voice. Resist the temptation to impersonate others to inject humor into the speech at someone else's expense.

Writing dialogue.

Don't write out dialogue! Only speak dialogue that you already remember clearly (if not precisely).

If you write it out, you will try to memorize it. If you try to memorize it, you will sound monotonous and defeat the purpose of including dialogue in the first place.

STORY DYNAMICS

If you believe that you have a good case to make in your message, then you have a good story to tell. You just have to find it.

From ancient times, many courtroom traditions have included an opening statement in legal cases, which is sometimes referred to as the *narrative*. Each attorney presents their story of the case to be heard. This is a suggested framework that the jury is invited to accept as a compelling account of the evidence to be presented in court.

Think of your message like a case, and put the message into a coherent story form that is faithful to the ideas and supporting material. The resulting story or scenario should put the emphasis of your message on people—how the message matters in practical terms for listeners in their lives.

What if someone asks, "Shouldn't we be using reasoning and argumentation instead of stories?" In fact, stories follow a strict logic. But it is a practical logic of listening and speaking, not an abstract logic of literacy or mathematics.

Story form is a friend of truth and logic. The most ardent and eloquent defenders of wisdom rely on stories more than isolated logical propositions and bare abstractions. Besides, stories require careful discernment in listening and speaking. A story is not a hedge against deceit. As Alasdair McIntyre has related, there are good stories and bad stories, true stories and false ones.

Story form is so powerful that speakers may be tempted to tell stories as a gimmick. Stories can be seductive for speakers. For instance, when listeners' eyes glaze over or close altogether, telling a relevant story often gets them re-engaged. Holding an audience's attention and knowing you are getting through to listeners can be intoxicating.

So never tell a story for its own sake. Never tell a story merely as an audience attention trick! A good story can start a speech and lead into the message. Just make sure that a story really belongs within the speech; only use ones that fit and advance the message.

Stories in Speeches: Oral Patterns in Speech Practice

We aren't telling a story instead of giving a speech. Stories are valuable elements in speeches. But we really want to use story dynamics to apply oral patterns in practice.

Find the plot and follow the plot line.

Start with the basic storyline of the message. How does the message emerge with reference to the people involved, including the audience?

Plot drives a good speech (not organization). Good stories are propelled by some issue or problem that affects people. Likewise, good speeches address problems, imperfections, or uncertainties that link the lives of speakers and audiences. Problems generate tension and direction for people—a reason to speak with purpose. The plot of the speech may be momentary or momentous, it may deal with joy or distress, but the world of the spoken word is dynamic. It invites us to engage listeners in the middle of lives already on the move.

Consider how the message develops as a progression of episodes. Each episode will suggest motives, decisions, and implications to speak about. Episodes lend themselves to story forms that can propel you into oral patterns that will come to life for listeners, whether true stories or tall tale, parables or case studies, scenarios or personal accounts. A good episode effectively integrates message content and capsulizes plot, drama, characters, and conversation. The purpose? To help people listen well and engage the message.

Find the drama.

What's at stake for listeners? We speak because an important event or decision for listeners has happened, is happening, or is going to happen.

Focus on the action in the message.

Action, not information, drives a good speech. Oral patterns concentrate on the human dimensions—particularly action that matters in our lives. Stories and story dynamics place human choices, decisions, and deeds front and center in our speeches. Where's the action for the audience in the message? Does the message itself call for action?

We enjoy listening to ordinary conversations about unresolved issues: who might lose their job? When's the storm supposed to hit? How do you find a good...(doctor, lawyer, plumber, school, church, neighborhood, etc.)? Use language that involves the audience in the crucial action and events of the message. Highlight tensions facing the audience, and their specific decisions and courses of action.

Listen for dialogue.

Who is involved in conversation within the message? People love to hear what people say and how they say it. Intense exchange, hushed discussion, cool contempt, hot debate, and witty banter all make for good listening. As you identify people relevant to your message, learn to hear their voices and bring those voices into the speech.

Put people in the messages as participants.

People, not material, drive a good speech. Oral patterns involve people-in-action, whether in stories or in our speeches. What people are involved in the message directly? Indirectly? Whether through story forms or dialogue, keep people and voices at the center of your speech as it develops. The people can make the message come alive.

Speak as a moral agent.

A good speech enacts embedded morals. Not every story has a "moral" per se, but as speakers we advance messages that invite evaluation on moral and ethical planes because listening and speaking are moral activities. When messages, decisions, and actions matter to listeners, the moral and ethical features of a speech leap to the foreground. Oral patterns feature these dimensions by enhancing our ability to speak and calling listeners to respond morally and ethically, even when the implications seem relatively modest.

Extend your range of oral performance.

> *Stories engage us as speakers.* The more we rely on oral patterns of thought and use story dynamics in our speech, the more interesting we become to listeners. There are two basic reasons. First, we tend to be more dynamic speakers, more natural, when telling stories. When we get into telling a story, we become more expressive. Second, stories enhance our memory for the message and important details without rote memorization. Gaining experience with both expression and oral memory can extend our skills in these areas to all aspects of our speaking, not just stories.

Why Stories? Make Content Memorable

Stories are memory machines. If you want people to remember something, put it in a story form. You can remember the essential elements of hundreds of good stories that you've heard just once. A good story in a speech puts the message in a powerful memory context.

People love to hear a good story. Good stories include oral dynamics that make the spoken word distinctive and memorable. Great speakers know that "Once upon a time…", "It was a dark and stormy night…", and "Lend me your ear…" are but a few of the phrases and tones that spark a special kind of interest within an audience. Audiences also respond to "Did you hear what…did?" or "Did you hear what happened to…yesterday?" They're hoping for something more interesting than the third bullet point in a seven-point bullet list.

To become good speakers we have to become good at basic storytelling. We don't have to become great storytellers in our own right—memorizing famous stories or folk tales, writing our own stories, or learning the entire art and craft of storytelling. To become good speakers we need to become fluent in the principles and practices of the spoken word.

And the best place to start is with "Once upon a time…"

Ideas in context.

> *A story tells where an idea comes from and how it fits in listeners' world.* When you tell a story, you offer mental links to other concrete ideas and experiences people have in mind.

Illustrations.

A story creates a mental image to explain what an idea means. Stories help us picture ideas. A story is an extended word picture directly involving audience memory and imagination.

Implications.

A story shows applications of an idea, how it works in the context of listeners' day-to-day lives. In practice, you can drive a point home through stories. Listeners, following more closely, will often beat you to the conclusion and beyond.

Where Stories Belong in a Speech

Public speaking is much more than storytelling, but it pays to understand the principles and forms that make stories work. Rely on story forms within a speech:

Introduction or conclusion.

Get the audience's attention and provide closure. A good, basic story is so appealing to most listeners that it is a great way to begin and/or end a speech. When you open with a good story, you engage the audience and get the message out early. When you end with a story, you provide listeners with closure and reinforce the message.

Supporting example.

Tell a brief story to illustrate a main theme or idea in the message. When you use a story as an example, keep it simple. Avoid digressions. You aren't telling the story for its own sake, but to strengthen the larger message.

Message thread.

Follow a story through the whole message to provide coherence and direction. You can digress from the story to build your case and develop other forms of support as well. Then pick up the story and continue through the next segment of the message.

Story Forms

Frame the point and main ideas in the message within story forms. Speakers can apply the basic principles that make stories both easy on the ears and easy to remember using a number of forms, including:

Accounts.

Records of people-in-action during specific past events or incidents. Accounts, because they involve real people and events, are crucial elements in many speeches. An account is a more dramatic element than mere description or reporting about the past. As a story forms, accounts focus our attention on the human dimensions–past and present–pertinent to our message for the audience.

- History. A historical account may provide recent background to an ongoing issue in the speech, or may provide an example from deeper in the past.

- Biography. The account may be personal, whether giving an account from our own life or using someone else's life and experience in the message.

- Eyewitnesses. We may have an official record or bring in a story from a recent conversation with someone who has given an eyewitness account that matters in the speech.

Scenarios.

Invent a story that will help listeners imagine an idea or message in a specific situational context. A scenario is a mental construct designed to create a mental diagram or "video" to make connections for listeners.

- Hypotheticals. Create a vision of a specific situation under certain conditions in story form.

  In speech, hypotheticals are mostly about, "What might happen?"[6]

  You can use a hypothetical as a kind of thought experiment with the audience, to play out possible consequences or applications of

[6]Hypotheticals can also take the present form–"What might be happening?"–and the past form–"What might have happened?"

a point or a proposition. To be helpful to speakers and audiences, the conditions assumed in a hypothetical scenario must be realistic, reasonable, and well supported.

Best-case/worst-case scenarios are forms of hypotheticals. They work particularly well in speeches that present proposals.

> "We always start by working from a worst-case scenario. Worst case, if we go with this proposal, it would look like this...On the other hand, the potential upside–the best-case scenario–is excellent. Our best-case scenario looks like this..."

Best-case/worst-case scenarios are most effective when they are realistic and correspond with the evidence in the message. Beware of the temptation to exaggerate. Hyperbole in a best-case/worst-case scenario can kill your credibility.

- Composites. Create a representative construct that combines a number of variables or experiences into a common story.

A composite simplifies predominant elements to provide explanations, or profiles and patterns. You can use a composite to develop interpretations and expectations for listeners. A composite scenario is a kind of summary in story form. It is a generalization that acts like a story so people can better envision what they're thinking about with the speaker through the message.

For example, instead of giving ten different examples, you create one:

What's the problem with driving while texting?

You're driving down the highway and there are ten cars close to you. At least two or three of the drivers are texting. You're approaching construction a few hundred yards ahead and the lanes narrow. There are concrete "New Jersey barriers." A construction sign says NO SHOULDER NEXT TWO MILES. Just before you get to the narrow road, one of the texters behind you begins to swerve into your lane at 65 mph, just as you slow down to navigate the barriers. There's no room to maneuver. You become a statistic.[7]

[7]http://investorplace.com/2014/06/texting-driving-statistics-2014/#.VVdiQPlVhBc May 16, 2015.

Speakers must tell listeners that they are working from a composite. To present a composite as an actual scenario is a deceit.

Parables.

A simple story used to teach virtues of practical wisdom. Parables can be found in most cultural traditions. Parables include folk tales and familiar groups of stories like Aesop's Fables, Hasidic tales, and the parables of Jesus Christ.

Parables aren't simple stories, they are simple stories with an edge. They often remind us of things we don't want to hear—even if we agree with the parable. The parable form connects with listeners forcefully; we hear clearly.

Practical wisdom uses parables to teach ideas and virtues that aren't difficult to understand, but that remind us of things that may be difficult to do in the moment. We sometimes would prefer to be exempt from their moral force.

When we consider ourselves powerful, we may look down on ordinary morality and practical ethics. When we consider ourselves intellectually sophisticated, we may look down on ordinary morality and practical ethics. Any time we want to pursue our immediate desires at the expense of others (or to take the punishment of others into our own hand by retaliation or revenge), we may look down on ordinary morality and practical ethics.

Wisdom speaks through parables to call our bluff.

A parable works like a metaphor. It uses familiar characters, figures, and situations designed to help us apply the message to our lives. The parable may not always apply directly to us, but everyone in the world of the parable "gets it," whether they want to or not.

Finding Stories

We have access to many stories. We don't need to try to learn new ones for a speech. Instead, we need to learn how to use what we already know.

First, we have direct personal experiences and plenty of observations. Use these experiences directly or as a basis for scenarios or parables. Second, we know many stories and scenes from what we have heard, read, or viewed, such as stories told to us, or relayed through books, music, movies, and plays. All are good sources of stories. Third, new material is rarely brand new or completely original. Many of our favorite books, movies, and songs are indebted to older ones, if they are not direct knock-offs or remakes.

Listeners love to hear stories. Speakers don't need to be expert storytellers to get across the value of a story in their speech. Speakers just need to make sure that their stories connect the message to the audience's world.

Tell the Story, Not *About* the Story

A good story, well told, is a gift to the audience.

In public speaking, good stories connect the message clearly to the audience. A good story brings action, events, dialogue, drama, and direction to a speech—all things that resonate and actively invite listeners into the message. The message comes to life and the audience becomes the center of attention in the speech.

Time passes fast for speakers and listeners when a good story is being told. People are doing things. Events are happening. Tensions rise and fall. Listeners encounter dilemmas and challenges, questions, and comic relief.

Often, speakers give a description of a story instead of telling it.

Telling about a story robs the audience of intrigue, interest, and the mental pleasure of thinking along with the speaker. When we tell about a story, listeners don't feel the message come to life—they feel like they are being talked to death. Telling about a story is more like a form of reading, which is based on the written word and radically different from good speaking. Reading so that it doesn't sound like you are just reading aloud is an art form called oral interpretation. Few speakers know this art. When you tell about a story, the audience gets droning descriptions instead of seeing and hearing it for themselves. Telling about a story makes the speaker the center of attention, not the audience. Time can't pass fast enough.

As scholars of orality, oral cultures and oral tradition have long taught us that storytelling is a great model for oral patterns, principles, and practices. Ordinary people use story forms in ordinary conversation almost every day. The challenge is to transform our conversational storytelling skills into use in public speaking.

Just go ahead and TELL the STORY!

Telling about a Story - Written Pattern	**Telling a Story - Oral Pattern**
I have a story I would like to tell you, if you like stories. The story is about this mean creature who lived on a mountain and hated all the little people who lived in a village down in the valley below. But before I tell you the story, I should tell you that it isn't a true story, but it is about a true kind of thing that can happen to people when they realize what other people are like, instead of relying on prejudices. So, in the story, the mean creature hates all the little people living in their village and loving each other. And the monster hates it most at holiday time. Why the mean creature, I think he's called "The Grinch," hates the little people isn't clear, but he does. So he finally has had enough of these people and their holiday traditions and he decides he's got to do something drastic to put an end to it.	Every *Who* Down in *Who*-ville Liked Christmas a lot... But the Grinch, Who lived just north of *Who*-ville Did NOT! The Grinch *hated* Christmas! The whole Christmas season! Now, please don't ask why. No one quite knows the reason. It *could* be his head wasn't screwed on just right. It *could* be, perhaps, that his shoes were too tight. But I think that the most likely reason of all May have been that his heart was two sizes too small. But, Whatever the reason, His heart or his shoes, He stood there on Christmas Eve, hating the *Whos*, Staring down from his cave with a sour, Grinchy frown At the warm lighted windows below in their town. For he knew every *Who* down in *Who*-ville beneath Was busy now, hanging a mistletoe wreath. "And they're hanging their stockings!" he snarled with a sneer. "Tomorrow is Christmas! It is practically here!" Then he growled, with his Grinch fingers nervously drumming, "I MUST find some way to stop Christmas from coming!"[8]

[8]Dr. Suess, *How the Grinch Stole Christmas* (New York:Random House,1985).

Story Form Pitfalls:

Missing the point.

Beware of "good stories" peripheral to the message. In any form, the story should support the proposition of the speech and the reasoning in the message.

Amusement.

Tell stories for the sake of the message, not to entertain speaker or listeners. People respond to stories. Work against the temptation to enjoy holding an audience's attention and to entertain yourself.

Self-absorbed storytelling.

Tell stories about yourself rarely and with great care. Keep your focus on the audience. You aren't nearly as interesting to listeners as you think you are.

ORAL PATTERN EXERCISES

Basic format.

In this set of exercises, speakers select or are assigned stories to tell.

The speaker needs to tell the story in 2-3 minutes. The story must include some spoken dialogue.

Purpose.

To stimulate oral patterns of thought for presentation by incorporating people-in-action and by performing dialogue.

Telling a story as part of a speech, even moderately well, connects audiences with the message personally. It helps speakers learn to use better vocal dynamics among other conversational, oral patterns.

Activities.

The three story telling exercises suggested below can be used as starting points from which to learn to integrate stories into your speeches. Use a one to three minute time limit.

1. A Favorite Story as a Kid...and Why.

   Tell a key part of a story that was a favorite story of yours as a kid. Tell the story from memory or give an updated paraphrase, including the voices of at least a person or two (real person or character). Anything from a true story about you to a story parents told you or a story book you loved. Make sure you tell why you loved the story.

2. A Recent Event from Which You Learned.

   Tell a story of a recent incident from which you learned a good, simple lesson. The lesson doesn't need to be life-changing, but the story should seem noteworthy to you. (e.g. I was stopped for passing a school bus with flashing red lights and learned how strict the penalty is...before the police officer chose not to cite me! You lose your license for six months, plus a hefty fine. Ouch!) Include the voices of key participants in a dialogue that happened during the event (such as the brief conversation with the police officer).

3. An Inter-generational Family Story.

   Tell a story from your grandparents' generation—a repeated family story that explains something important about your family's history that affects what you believe. The story has to include voices from your family in the telling of it. (e.g. My grandfather always said, "You've always got to be able to walk away from a major purchase, you never have to buy today, or else you will get taken.")

Lead with Content 3

Saying Something; to Someone; about Something[1]

[1]This is an application of the idea of communicative praxis as explained by Calvin O. Schrag, *Communicative Praxis and the Space of Subjectivity*, (Indiana University Press, 1989)32-47.

Your message–the content–is for the audience, not for you.

The primary reason to speak in public is to communicate something that matters within the lives of the audience. The priority is to engage listeners and to invite a substantial response.

Good speaking starts with a message worthy of the audience's full attention. As listeners, we know that good speakers connect us to things that really matter. Poor speakers never make a connection...and we tune them out.

Therefore, direct the message toward the audience; help them "get it" and make sense of the message in their world.

PURPOSE: *To identify a clear point and develop strong reasoning with support for your message.*

PRINCIPLE: *The content of the message drives the quality of the speech.*

PRACTICE: *Content speeches.*

GET TO THE POINT OF THE SPEECH

"What's the point?" As listeners, this is our prime question. But so many speakers never seem to get to the point. As speakers, we need a good, direct answer to the "what's the point?" question.

We need an answer to be said, not read. In other words, the point of the speech needs to be "sayable."

The point also needs to be memorable. This point, easy to say, needs to be memorable for listeners and not just for you. When you get to the simple "sayable" that captures your purpose and sticks in your mind easily, good message design will flow better. The rest of your work will make better sense. After all, you're preparing to speak, not writing an essay to be "delivered on its hind legs."[2]

[2]A favorite quote from Carroll Arnold related by Douglas J. Pedersen, longtime mentor and professional friend of public speaking teachers at Penn State University–University Park.

How to Find the Point

Your job is to locate the content of your message within the audience. You are trying to place the message within their world and put it into language that will resonate with them.

Work through the stock categories and questions below carefully. You can move quickly, but don't take shortcuts. Think through each one with care...and keep working. Don't stop to ponder.

Assess the rhetorical situation.[3]

[3]Lloyd F. Bitzer, "The Rhetorical Situation," *Philosophy & Rhetoric* 1, no.1 (1968):1-14.

Explore the arrangements. Obviously you want to think through basic questions like time and place, speaking venue, time limits, larger agenda, audience size and makeup, etc. With this basic information in place, you can turn to more important questions of content development below.

- Active Audience: Who are the listeners that need your message?

The purpose of the speech must be tied to listeners who can do something in response to your speech. Ignore people with no stake in the situation. Address decision-makers, not spectators.

- Speaker: Why are you speaking?

Your role is a big factor in what you say!

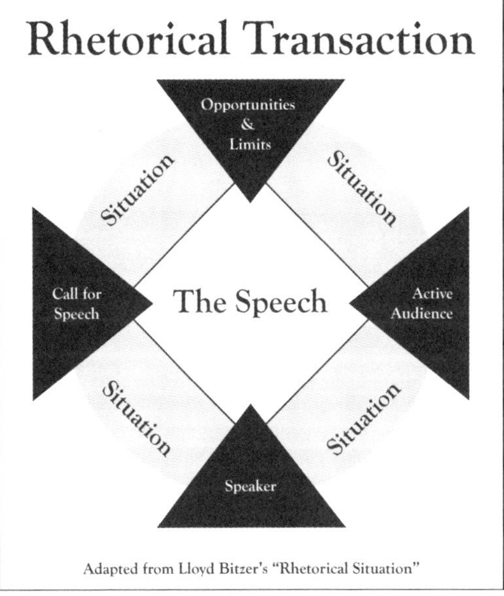

Adapted from Lloyd Bitzer's "Rhetorical Situation"

Consider both what you have to bring to the rhetorical situation and the audience's expectations for a message from you in the specific situation.

- Call for Speech: Why does the speech need to be given?

  The content of the speech should resolve a problem—or contribute to the situation in some other way—whether there's new information, a simple problem, a crisis, or a celebration. Match the message to the need; the speech needs to fit the rhetorical situation.

- Opportunities and Limits: Why here and now?

  What can and must be said? What must not be said? The call, the audience, and the speaker intersect to open some doors and close other doors, each of which affect what you can say and how you can say it. Look to capitalize on openings and respect constraints.

Find the central question.

What's the audience asking you? (Or what should they be asking you?) Think of your speech as a response to a question that comes from the audience. Use the basic questions below to get to a set of questions you can use as a starting point.

- Who, What, Where, When? *These questions lead to facts and definitions.*
- Why? *This question leads to causes, intentions, and motives.*
- So What? *This question leads to effects, implications, and consequences.*
- What Now? What Next? *These questions lead to decisions.*
- How? *This question leads to processes and implementation.*

Which questions are closest to your purpose in speaking to this particular audience in this specific situation? Which ones will be most important to listeners?

First limit yourself to the top 2-3 questions, then decide which one is the top priority. Your central question should lead to a strong point on which to build your speech.

Hear the central question as a common question.

The central question resides in the audience; it's not the speaker's question.

The question must resonate with listeners. A good speaker meets the audience in the question. Every listener should be able to understand and connect with the question. That's what it means to make the central question a common question. There may or may not be a common answer–that's not crucial. (In some cases you may want a spectrum of answers.) Good questions help listeners engage the message actively and prompt a variety of thoughtful responses.

When the central question of the speech is a common question, the starting point is shared by speaker and audience. The question focuses audience attention. This is not to make listeners think what speakers want them to, but to help speakers and listeners think well together.

Draft a preliminary point.

Answer the central question in a way that makes good sense to you.

What do you want the audience to believe in reference to the question?

Put your response in your own words. Don't worry at first about the form. Get the initial thought–the central idea–in place. Keep your mind fixed on the idea in relation to the audience, but say it in a way that makes sense to you. To speak well, you have to have full command of the point.

A Question of Purpose: Informative vs. Persuasive

Human speech has a persuasive tendency. "Language is sermonic," as Richard Weaver said.[4] When we speak, we invite people to adopt a particular view of the world. So technically, we could say that there's no such thing as an "informative" speech. But practically, many speakers are simply trying to get a basic message across. So perhaps there are informative speeches after all!

[4]Richard M. Weaver, "Language is Sermonic," *Language is Sermonic: Richard M. Weaver on the Nature of Rhetoric.* eds. Richard L. Johannesen, et al. (Louisiana State University Press, 1970).

In practice, knowing whether a message is informative or persuasive is about what you are asking listeners to do. When the content that listeners will receive is non-controversial, we approach the message in an informative way. When the point is to invite a pronounced change in degree or direction—to decide, to move, or to act—we approach the message in a more persuasive way.

Basic speech purposes.

Draft the point with the purpose of the speech in mind.

Consider the primary purpose of your speech. The reasons we speak involve more than simple information or persuasion, and a single speech may accomplish a number of purposes. The goal of your speech is to focus on an emphasis, informative or persuasive, and keep the emphasis clear. The speech can go badly if you hope to persuade people but speak as though you were merely teaching them new content.

- To Understand: You want the audience to understand the content of the message. An informative speech presents important ideas in a non-controversial manner. The purpose is to teach, not to persuade.

- To Decide: You want the audience to agree with an idea, position, or proposal you are advocating. Classic persuasive speeches ask the audience to make a specific judgment in a decision-making context.

- To Motivate: You want the audience to believe more strongly something about which they are already convinced. The purpose of many persuasive speeches is to intensify commitment, belief, and existing attitudes.

- To Take Action: You want the audience to take a specific action and to do so for a specific reason. Some persuasive speeches involve a direct call for action. The call is for swift action—right now! *Not some day...*

How to Refine the Point

Once you've drafted a preliminary point, your message is stated in its first form. From this first response, you need to craft the point of the speech in a way that makes sense to listeners.

Direct and sharpen the preliminary point.

Revise to strengthen message and listener connections.

When you actually speak the point of the message for listeners, you've got to reach them in their own context for maximum impact.

- Keep It Simple. Make the point a concise, direct statement.

  The point must answer the stock audience question, "What's the point?" It must be concise and easy to say. No clauses, asides, qualifications, or conditions.

  Your first job is to help the audience "get" the message with ease. Think of the point as a "hook" that announces the basic message and purpose of the speech. With the point in place, you can develop the message by hanging the details on the point that's secure in the mind of listeners.

- State the Point in Positive Terms. Avoid negatives and rely on constructive language.

  Listeners process constructive wording more easily than negative language.[5] A commonly repeated formula says that thinking through a negative takes ten times as long as thinking through a positive. Using negative phrases can be important and good in a speech. So don't try to change every negative into a positive. Rather, when you're crafting your point, focus on telling us what we should believe and do. Remember that we get our minds around a "yes" more quickly and easily than a "no."

- Frame the Point within Audience Priorities. Give listeners "handles" for immediate recognition.

  Make the point in a way that connects to listeners' present circumstances and concerns. They should understand why the point is vitally important in their current situation. Expect to

[5]Jonathan Price and Lisa Price, *Hot Text: Web Writing that Works*, (Pearson, 2003), 222-225.

continue to refine the point as you craft the message. Aim to get the point into shape so that when listeners hear it, they never ask, "What do they mean by that?"

- Put the Point in Resonant Terms. Restate the point with the ears of the audience in mind.

  The point should sound good to listeners, be easy to say, and easy to recall. For a technical audience, use jargon; for a general audience, simplify; for a formal occasion, use formal language; for informal contexts, keep a light touch.

  Work with the flow of the point until the words have a good "feel" as you speak. When a phrase feels right, you'll be able to say it in a way that sticks in the mind of the listener.

- Invite Response. Frame the point in a thought provoking way that stimulates discussion.[6]

  Craft your response to the central question in a way that involves listeners in a real dialogue. Although you are working more formally than casual conversation, messages and responses flow simultaneously between listeners and speakers. From the start, the message should spark further conversation.

[6]Mikhail M. Bakhtin, *Speech Genres & Other Late Essays*, (Austin: University of Texas Press, 1986), 68-70.

Point Pitfalls

Finding the point allows you to put the message into words and shapes the content of the rest of the speech. Therefore, beware of the following pitfalls:

Don't miss the point.

The topic is not the point!

If you have too much to say, or don't have enough to say, you don't have a real point yet.

Don't miss the audience.

Touch the lives of listeners.

If the point hits audience members where they live, they're more likely to "get" the speech.

Don't miss the question.

With no common question to tie together the topic and audience, you can't find the point.

Good questions drive important speeches. Weak questions produce rambling speeches, bored listeners, and dry speakers.

REASON WITH THE AUDIENCE

An audience will take the speech more seriously when you have clear, strong reasons. With good reasons, listeners can convince themselves and others that your message is worthwhile. The audience makes the message its own.

Audiences Ask For Good Reasons

Listeners need good reasons to believe your message. Stephen Toulmin notes that listeners tend to ask three basic types of questions that speakers can use to find support for the message we present in a speech.[7]

[7]Stephen Toulmin, *The Uses of Argument*, (New York, NY: Cambridge University Press, 1995), 1-8; 97-99.

- Basic Reasons: What makes you say so?

  What are the most obvious reasons and evidence that support the message of your speech?

- Inference: How does the evidence support your opinion?

  Why do you think that the basic reasons support the opinions you have stated? How are you making this inference?

- Background: Why should I believe what you say?

  What are deeper reasons and evidence behind the basic reasons and inferences that support your opinion?

Toulmin makes a simple point: People listen for the "soundness" of our reasons—is the message well-supported, credible, and trustworthy? (See "coherence" and "fidelity" in Chapter 1: Ethics in Public Speaking.)

How to Find Good Reasons

You're looking for reasons why the audience should believe and adopt the message. First develop a surplus of reasons from which to build the content of your message.

Record your own reasons.

Why do you believe the message?

Sometimes you're so involved in the work and content that you forget to analyze your own reasoning!

The best starting point is your own rationale for the point and message. Make a list.

Anticipate audience questions.

What questions will the audience ask—what questions should the audience ask?

List probable questions—ones that you have already heard related to your message. Note the best questions that could be asked, even if you don't expect them to come up. (You'll repeat this exercise when working with objections.)

Raising a tough question and providing a good answer can enhance the credibility of the message for listeners.

Think on your feet: Inventing good reasons.

What practical reasons can you generate through a system of topical invention?

People have been thinking on their feet since ancient times by learning basic prompts to work through familiar categories, topics (*topoi*), or common places (*loci*) in our minds. Ancients like Aristotle, Cicero, and Boethius detailed categories and created specialized lists. Our list is a starter-set based on this tradition. Once you learn it, you can use it in all kinds of situations.

Topical invention is a leave-no-stone-left-unturned method of practical reasoning. Topical systems build your creativity. They can cause some brain pain at first, but the work will pay off with greater mental agility and stronger reasoning in everyday situations.

A topical invention system uses basic thought questions–topical prompts–to train your mind to find reasons. While working through the prompts, remember that you're finding ideas, not answers.

Work fast. Part of the process is to find practical reasons others will recognize too. Don't overthink it. If you don't get a good reason pretty quickly, move on to the next prompt.

- <u>A Note on "It" in a Topical Invention System.</u>

  To use a topical system, you need a "placeholder" for your point (like a variable [x] in a mathematical equation). In many systems, the placeholder is "it".

  But what is "it"? The "it" is what you're trying to find reasons about.

  If your point is that people have become slaves to cell phones, then "it" would be cell phone slavery.

TOPICAL INVENTION SYSTEM PROMPTS

Topical Category: RELATIONSHIP

The Point: *People are enslaved to their cell phones.*

What is its cause?	*Affordable, portable, digital, communication devices with Internet access.*
What is its effect?	*Distraction. Poor interpersonal communication.*
What preceded it? (*not caused it*)	*Landlines. Internet. Old mobile phones.*
What happened after it? (*not caused by it*)	*"Miniturization." Expanded features.*
What is an alternative to it?	*Cell phone slaves see no alternatives.*
What is its complement?	*Internet slavery.*

Topical Category: CIRCUMSTANCE

It is possible/impossible?	*Widely. Cell phone availability is high.*
Is it likely/unlikely?	*The nature of cell phones invites slavery.*
Is it practical/impractical?	*Very. Accepted/expected everyday practice.*
Is it desirable/undesireable?	*Slaves find it intoxicating.*
Is it necessary/unnecessary? Beneficial/harmful?	*Unnecessary.* *Harmful to persons and communities as commonly used today.*
Did it exist previously?	*No. Never in this form.*
Will it exist in the future?	*Yes. But not in its current form.*

Topical Category: FACT

Does it exist?	*Yes. Cell phone slavery does exist.*

Topical Category: DEFINITION

What is it? Is it part of a larger class (genus)?	*Yes. Addiction.*
Is it part of a smaller class (species)?	*Yes. Media addictions.*

Topical Category: QUALITY

What is its nature?	*Cell phones control some people.*

What are its characteristics?	*Users respond to cell phones as top priority.*
Topical Category: COMPARISON	
What is it most like?	*A master who must be obeyed.*
What is it similar to?	*Uncontrolled Internet use.*
What is it different from?	*Secret addictions—it's public.*
How does it compare in degree (more, less, equal)?	*Worse than Internet because it's mobile and disrupts others.*
Topical Category: DIVISION	
What is it identified with?	*Personal media. Media sophistication. Popular fashion.*
What is distinctive about it?	*Interactive. More common. More distracting. Pervasive.*
Topical Category: TESTIMONY	
Who said it according to what authority?	Neil Postman in *Technopoly.*
Who said it according to what experience?	Thomas de Zengotita in *Meditated*
Who sait it according to what research?	Nicholas Carr in *The Shallows: What the Internet Is Doing to Our Brains.*
What said it according to what wisdom?	Walter Ong in *Orality & Literacy.*
Who said it according to what evidence?	Quentin Schultze in *Habits of the High-Tech Heart.*
Who said it according to what law?	Jacques Ellul in *The Technological System.*
Who said it according to what precedent?	Aldous Huxley in *Brave New World.*
Who said it according to what policy?	Marketing executives for major cell phone technology, according to *Advertising Age.*
Who said it according to what record?	Accounts of teens and young adults attesting to cell phone dependence as recorded in extensive news and sociological reports and studies.
Who said it according to what tradition?	Kenneth Burke, in "The Definition of Man," in *Language as Symbolic Action*

How to Refine Good Reasons

Sort through the reasons you have generated and pick the ones that will connect your message to the audience in their lives.

Categorize.

Organize your reasons in groups that make sense to you. Employ trains of thought that fit together.

Rank.

Prioritize the reasons according to which ones offer the audience the best rationale for adopting the point.

- Audience. Which reasons are closest to the interests, knowledge, and experience of this particular audience? What reasons do they need most to understand the message?

- Occasion. What reasons are most important in this context? What fits the situation best?

- Speaker. What reasons are enhanced by your role in the situation? What will listeners be able to hear best from you...and not?

Select.

As you consider which reasons to use, choose ones that:

- Respond to Expectations. Good reasons tell listeners where the point originates from, where it's going, and why they should follow. Offer a train of thought that makes your speech worth the audience's attention.

- Make Listeners Think. Good reasons stimulate careful thought about the message. What are the more thought-provoking reasons you can offer?

- Resonate with Experience. Good reasons strike a chord that produces easy audience recognition. A reason can sound new as long as it harmonizes well with listeners' modes of thought and fits their basic sensibilities. It's what they know, not what you think they should know!

- Demonstrate Coherence. The audience expects a reasonable case that holds together. Your good reasoning builds audience confidence in the integrity and good sense of your message.

- Invite Scrutiny. The audience wants reasons that stand up to questioning. Will your reasons stand under pressure? Can you give good responses to tests by thoughtful listeners? If so, your message will benefit greatly–good reasons stand up to the test.

We want our messages to be taken seriously, even when people raise doubts or concerns. Consider scrutiny as a compliment. Audiences discount a lot of speakers! So welcome public scrutiny. Being ignored is the worst form of objection.

Deciding What To Say

What can/cannot be said?

Time, knowledge, and language all limit what you can say.

Some things in the speaking situation are beyond your control. What options are open and closed to you in this situation?

What must be said?

To make the point and message clear, you simply must say certain things.

The point is the core of the message. You need certain reasons to support it with the audience. Which reasons are crucial?

What must not be said?

Particular audiences and occasions make it impossible to say certain things, even true things.

Laws, expectations, common courtesy, and the array of knowledge levels in the audience are all factors that prevent us from saying certain things. What must be ruled out for this message?

What should be said?

Conditions and the particular orientation of an audience make certain reasons high priorities.

You need supporting reasons that reinforce the validity and coherence of the message for the specific group of listeners. With the specific audience and occasion in mind, which reasons should you include?

What should not be said?

Some reasons or approaches to reasoning (such as subtle deceits) might work, but would violate ethics and practical wisdom.

In the most difficult cases, we may be tempted to use reasons that we either believe to be true, but are unsupported; are likely to be true, but are unsubstantiated; or the audience is likely to receive as being true on the occasion, but without evidence. What should you reject?

What may be said?

If you've done good work, a broad scope of legitimate "sayable" reasons will remain.

What other reasons will most help listeners get the message?

Reason Pitfalls

Opinions alone.

An opinion without a good reason behind it is just an assertion.

Good reasons are necessary to move a message beyond mere opinion. "Just because..." or "because I said so..." are inadequate responses to listener questions. If you don't have good reasons, audiences shouldn't listen or take you seriously.

Mistaking information for reasons.

Listeners need rationale.

A large volume of data or other evidence by itself is not enough. Information can support good reasons (see chapter 8), but audiences need reasons to make the connections that give the message meaning.

Faulty reasons.

Avoid fallacies or diversions of reasoning.[8]

Whether on purpose or by accident, speakers can lead an audience astray by using twisted reasoning—over-generalizing, personal attacks, appealing to emotion (instead of reason), or creating false dilemmas, to name a few.[9] Reasoning diversions do not hold up well under scrutiny, so reason with care!

[8]Edward P. J. Corbett and Rosa A. Eberly, *The Elements of Reasoning*, (Boston: Allyn & Bacon, 2000), 124-130.

[9]Karlyn Kohrs Campbell and Susan Schultz Huxman, *The Rhetorical Act* (Belmont, CA: Wadsworth, 2003), 120.

SUPPORT FOR YOUR REASONS

In public, nobody cares about your opinion! Uninformed, unsupported opinions and personal preferences exhaust us. By themselves, your assertions are worthless. If you're going to speak to us, give us some ground; give us some depth; give us some substance.

When you tie your opinion to good evidence, suddenly you become interesting...engaging...worth hearing. Well-supported opinions make for good listening and real value, even if we end up disagreeing.

Quality evidence strengthens the speech in many ways.

Build a good case.

Evidence always matters. The more important the speech, the more important the evidence.

This is as true for an informative speech as it is for a controversial speech. Quality evidence in an informative speech invites an audience to value the message more highly.

Raise the stakes for decision-makers.

Quality evidence appeals to listeners on their own terms.

Audiences need to consider the message from their own perspective. Strong support sparks interest in the speech as the content becomes more compelling.

Enhance your credibility.

Quality evidence cultivates respect. Through evidence, credible sources such as people, documents, organizations, and other sources of knowledge become contributors to the message. It's not all on you. Solid support shows you to be reliable, smart, and careful—well worth hearing.

How to Find Good Support

You have to be systematic and deliberate to generate quality support. Seek backing that will withstand scrutiny. Of your own evidence, become a harsher judge than your toughest critic.

To discover good evidence with limited time, work through a few basic questions:

What convinced you?

Spell out what you already know that supports the reasons behind the point you are making.

Why do you have confidence in your own reasons? Don't take the foundation of your reasons for granted. Remind yourself about the combination of reasoning and evidence that got you to the point of the speech in the first place.

What are your hunches?

Find the sources of supporting material that you "just know" are out there.

Recover and explore inklings, articles, or ideas that have dimmed in your memory. You're thinking that this organization—that author—this study—that historical document—has information or insights you need to make this case? Confirm promising leads that may produce quality evidence and document them. Go find the material you've not taken the time to locate.

Where can you find new material?

Search out new sources of evidence to support your case. Begin with leads from your more familiar sources of evidence.

We speak best about what we know best. So in most real-world cases your best evidence will come from prior knowledge, not new research. In many cases, new research will be essential for parts of the speech, and some situations call for us to generate a lot of new evidence.

- Prospects. Good support, whatever the form, comes by learning from other people.

Therefore, a basic research question is, "Who would know this and could help me learn about it?" Quality evidence often comes from the work of others. Find those who can teach you what you need to know in person or through other modes. Regardless of mode or manner, common standards for source quality apply:

1. ACCESS. Is the person or their work accessible to you and to the audience?
2. REVIEW. Has the work been evaluated by others who are qualified to assess its quality?
3. DOCUMENT. Can you cite sources that confirm the person's credibility to the satisfaction of listeners?

- Processes. Good research means getting as close as possible to the people from whom we need to learn.

Ultimately, a good research process is judged by the quality of the documented evidence produced. To gather evidence, you need to use basic modes of experiential learning: interviews, listening, reading, viewing, and documenting.

What Counts As Good Support?

Listeners looking for evidence ask: "Why should I believe you?"

Too often, speakers limit their idea of evidence to data, statistics or courtroom evidence. But good evidence comes from many kinds of sources in a wide array of fields. Standards for good evidence vary. Different things count as evidence in medicine than in business, in engineering than in law, in religion than in accounting, in music than in physics, and in psychology than in politics.

In some contexts, like a courtroom, rules of evidence are spelled out precisely; in other contexts, the rules are less formal. The practical question in every situation is: Will the evidence pass audience scrutiny?

Three basic sources are good starting points for evidence:

Documents.

Records of policy, performance, and practice.

What's already been said and done related to your message that's a matter of public record? Everything from federal law to an organization's stated policy to a person's public statement (in print or available electronically, including e-mail and Internet sources) count as public documentation.

Examples.

Inductive reasoning–reports from experience and research.

What exhibits can you find that support your message? Examples include personal experience, historical records, and published research studies.

Principles.

Deductive reasoning–practical wisdom accepted by the audience.

How does what people believe about the world support the message? Conventional wisdom, working rules, and established beliefs can serve as powerful sources of evidence.

Scrutinize Support at the Source

Qualify (or disqualify) all potential sources of evidence, including Internet sources, according to basic criteria:

Credibility.

Is the source reliable from the audience's standpoint?

Confirm the authenticity of the evidence, no matter where you find it. There is no instant credibility.

Relevance.

Is the source clearly connected to the message?

Weigh the proximity of the evidence to the point of the message. Don't waste time with interesting material that does not apply directly.

Fit.

Will the audience understand how the source supports the message?

Consider the degree to which the evidence suits the audience and occasion. It's only good evidence if the audience will get it.

Ultimately, the audience is the final judge of the evidence.

Techno-Mediocrity: The Allure of Internet Research

The Internet offers research tools that speakers can use to identify evidence. But the research potency of the Internet does not automatically produce good evidence. Speed enhances availability, but does not necessarily enhance quality.

Blind faith in the Internet can delude us into feeling that, "Because I am using the Internet, I am getting quality information faster!" Faith in the pseudo-authority of the Internet contributes to further research mediocrity. We may mistake unsubstantiated Internet material for good evidence, thinking, "Because I found this on the Internet, it is credible and authoritative." Finally, the temptation to use Internet research exclusively invites research mediocrity: "Only Internet sources are worthwhile; all other sources are invalid, irrelevant, and outdated."

There are no shortcuts to quality.

Therefore, use the Internet as one way to consult public documents, historical records, personal experiences, eyewitness accounts, books (fiction and non-fiction), research studies, magazines, newspapers, and professionals/scholars.

The mindset that all good evidence must be available via the Internet is deadly. The antidote for techno-mediocrity is not to abandon the Internet, but to apply established research principles and evaluation criteria to Internet sources and to use well-established Internet sources to supplement other high-quality sources of support.

How to Refine Support

If you do your research well, you should locate more backing and other evidence that you can use in the message.

As you refine your evidence, ask, "What counts as evidence for this audience, concerning this point, on this occasion?"

The process of deciding what evidence to use involves the following considerations:

Basic conditions.

Apply general criteria to evaluate the usefulness of the evidence you've gathered for the speech.

- Connected to Reasons. Audiences expect strong, obvious links between evidence and reasons.

  Good evidence provides a substantial base and a clear connection to reasons. Listeners take the message more seriously when there's a strong connection between evidence and reasoning.

- Independent of the Speaker. Listeners expect to hear more than the thoughts and experiences of the speaker alone.

  Good evidence provides a knowledge base that is easily available to the audience from other sources.

[10]For more on the importance of scrutinizing evidence, see Richard D. Rieke, Malcolm O. Sillars, and Tarla Rai Peterson, *Argumentation and Critical Decision Making, 6th ed.* (Addison-Wesley, 2004).

- Open to Scrutiny.[10] Audiences expect to be able to "inspect the evidence" to verify its quality and credibility.

  Good evidence can be confirmed by listeners. To be practical, the audience must be able to check out the evidence on their own.

Application.

Consider specific uses according to the message and audience.

- Organize and Prioritize Resources. Connect supporting materials to the appropriate parts of the message.

  Try to support every major reason in the speech with evidence. Linking reasons with evidence creates arguments. Prioritize available evidence from strongest to weakest.

- Review Relevance to the Audience. Think about how the evidence works within the context of the speech.

  How do different types of available evidence intersect with the audience's priorities and expectations?

  1) SITUATION & OCCASION. What counts as evidence in this context?

  Review standards and expectations of the audience to select the best evidence. Also consider how to prioritize evidence and still respect time constraints for the occasion. Respect audience composition and harmonize your supporting material with their needs and expectations.

  2) POINT. What support does the point demand specifically?

  The simple goal is to provide evidence that will help the audience to hear and respond well to the message. Confirm the evidence you know to be essential to support the point that drives the speech.

- Adopt Support That Best Fits The Case. Select backing to provide listeners with the best opportunity to get the message.

Give priority to the evidence that will generate the greatest credibility. Combine relevance, precision, and connection to the reasoning in the speech.

Support Pitfalls

Pay careful attention to details to develop strong backing. Common problems include:

Using easy support rather than good support.

Don't settle too quickly on the first sources of evidence you find.

Negligence with evidence can kill what might otherwise become a quality speech. Last minute searches often produce shoddy support—evidence that won't stand up.

Missing the audience.

Backing that does not connect to the audience provides no support at all.

If the audience doesn't connect, the speaker is at fault. Many sources of support will connect with many audiences, but sources should not be used if they will not advance the message with the specific listeners you're speaking to today.

Limiting forms of evidence.

Principles and examples meaningful to the audience are often more powerful than statistics and studies.

Don't get trapped relying on one form of support when many kinds of support are available and can be used well in most cases.

CONTENT DEVELOPMENT EXERCISE

Basic format.

In this set of exercises, speakers give a content-driven one-point speech with two reasons and support.

The speaker needs to give the one-point message in 2-3 minutes. The message must include the main point, two reasons, and backing for each reason.

Purpose.

To stimulate oral patterns of thought for presentation by incorporating people-in-action and by performing dialogue.

To make a good case, a message needs more than a point. The point needs to be supported by good reasons and substantial backing. The reasoning and support do not necessarily take long to state.

Activities.

The short speech exercises suggested below require selection of a simple point and two reasons with support. Use a three-minute time limit. For all three speeches...

- Use the topical invention system to find seven possible reasons. Pick two.
- For the selected reasons, find two different forms of backing for each one.
- Based on the work above, prepare a three-minute, one-point speech on one of the following topics:

   1. We should all learn...

      Fill in the blank with something that you think you and your listeners need to learn that would benefit them and people close to them. (e.g. a specific skill, a particular foreign language, a trade, specific knowledge, etc.)

   2. A great, uncommon gift to give that can't be bought...

Fill in the blank with a gift that listeners can/should give that cannot be bought with money. The gift needs to be commonly available, but uncommonly given.

3. We need to change... even though you won't hear about it on the Internet or TV.

   Fill in the blank with something that you think needs to change, but that is not typically in the popular mindset, whether in the news media, popular culture, or as a common topic in school/work. (e.g. how we think about children; eating alone; worrying about "–isms"; etc.).

Arrange by Ear 4

What's the Plot?

Drama is dramatic because people have to respond to unresolved difficulties. We watch intently as the plot thickens and human motives and decisions play out. Put the audience in a thick plot with dramatic tension they can feel in their own lives. Listeners have to decide how to respond in the situation.

Find the Dramatic Tension

Whether a case involves a group decision or a personal choice, finding the dramatic tension for listeners will give you a powerful answer to the common question, "Why should I listen to this speech—what's in it for me?" Feature the dramatic tension in the message and you'll help people respond well. Arrange to put content into context. *Audiences get the message when speakers address listener questions.* Drive your speech design with listener questions and you will earn audience attention.

Give good reasons to listen.

Why should I listen? A speech holds the audience's attention better when you respond to listener questions by design. We listen better when a speaker focuses on our own questions.

Intrigue the audience.

People enjoy hearing and thinking about problems. Problem solving processes invite listeners to think through ideas, options, and alternatives as you speak.

Provoke thoughtful attitudes and motives.

Challenge minds and hearts together. To move an audience, you have to reach more than the intellect. You have to engage the will. Both reason and emotion are necessary if listeners are going to make a decision and/or act.

PURPOSE: *To design speaking structures that are easy for listeners to follow by ear.*

PRINCIPLE: *If the speaker cannot remember the structure of the spoken word without notes, the audience will not be able to remember the message.*

PRACTICE: *Build speaking episodes on common speech structures.*

RESPOND TO QUESTIONS

When the situation calls for a speech, listeners have questions.

Public speaking moves people by building good responses to their questions. But they won't know they're getting good responses without organization that addresses their questions directly. Information alone rarely moves the will. We need clear motives to decide and act. Arrangement helps us unify thought, imagination, and emotion.

Good speakers take audience questions seriously. Through careful organization, they address what really matters, why it matters, and what we should do about it.

Prepare a Planned Conversation

Think of arranging a speech as planning a good conversation.

In everyday life, problems, questions, and challenges lead to meaningful discussions. When an important conversation comes up, you plan what you're going to say in advance and you anticipate the statements and questions of the other person. You can use the same kind of patterns in preparation and presentation.

- Asking for a Salary Increase

  When you plan a conversation with a boss about a salary increase, you might plan the conversation this way:

  You anticipate the boss's first question: "Why did you want to meet with me today?"

You've prepared an answer: "Since we're coming up on the end of the year, I wanted to talk with you about my compensation package."

You anticipate the boss's response: "Money is very tight this year. We shouldn't expect much more than a cost-of-living increase. (Implied question: "Why do you want a raise?")

You've done your homework and respond: "Yes. Money's tight. But I wanted to talk with you about a few concerns I have. First, the average salary level for people in my position and at the same career stage is 7% higher than my salary. Second, comparable employees in the organization make 5-10% more than I am currently making. And finally, I've had strong performance evaluations and competing organizations have expressed interest in having me work for them."

You anticipate the boss's question in response: "I see. But don't you like the working conditions here and our superior benefits program?"

You respond: "Yes. We have good benefits, but other firms have almost identical benefits and many have good working conditions too. A good friend of mine is working with one of them. I don't expect that you can raise my salary on the spot. I just wanted to let you know of my concerns before salary decisions were made for next year. Thanks!"

Whether you get the raise or not, you've prepared your conversation—just like you should prepare a speech. You've given organized support by anticipating audience questions.

THE IMPORTANCE OF QUESTIONS

Whoever asks the questions controls the conversation.

–Kenneth Burke

Which Questions Matter Most?

Consider what questions might be most prominent for listeners.

Starting points.

What's the point? Why are you speaking to us? Show relevance to the audience by organizing your speech to deal with these questions early and often. It's impossible to demonstrate relevance too soon.

Focus points.

What's most important? What's the problem? Give priority to audience attentionby organizing your speech as not to cover information, but to guide people to the crucial questions.

Decision points.

What do you want us to do about it? Highlight response options by organizing your speech to lead listeners to the best possible responses.

How to Find Specific Audience Questions

Anticipate audience questions to guide arrangement. Get audience questions in mind before you organize the speech formally. Think through the following scenarios:

Roundtable.

In a spontaneous conversation about your message with a few audience members, what questions might start the conversation? Think through the process of how each of your responses might invite another question.

Press conference.

> *If you were holding a press conference and the listeners were reporters, what questions and follow-ups might you anticipate?* Think about the questions that could come from different interests, perspectives, and concerns within the audience.

Live interview.

> *If you were being interviewed live by an audience member, what questions would they ask? In what order?* Script the interview from a good starting point for listeners. Why would they listen and what questions might a good interviewer use to organize the discussion?

The audience questions you find should harmonize with basic questions of starting points, focus points, and decision points. Remember, the questions come in response to your initiative—the main point of the message. The emphasis and order of questions should vary from one audience to another. You're trying to reach one specific audience with your basic message, not trying to find the message itself.

Organize with Questions

Arrange questions to feature the point of the speech. Good organization moves through questions that bring the audience to the heart of the message.

Type of question.

> *Audience questions suggest good structures.* The structures in Chapter 12 answer different types of questions. Prominent questions about the message that you anticipate from listeners will help you arrange the speech well.

Priority questions.

> *Audience questions suggest their priorities.* Organize the message to highlight the most important issues for your listeners.

Sequence of questions.

Audience questions suggest their pattern of logic. A good structure will help you match the progression of the speech to listener thinking. If you're going to think it through with them, you'll have to arrange the speech to match how they're thinking about it.

- Road Rage: Use Basic Listener Questions to Move Through the Message:

  1. *What's the problem?* Road rage (aggressive driving) is on the increase.
  2. *Why are we facing this problem?* Chronic underestimators do not allow enough travel time and don't want to miss their meetings and priorities.
  3. *What do you want me to do about it?* Keep a safe distance–don't engage rabid drivers. Take license numbers and report rabid drivers. Practice patience when you're behind schedule yourself.

Objections: A Useful Form of Question[1]

In the process of arranging the speech, objections provide a reality check. To craft messages with care, find counterarguments and take them seriously. What are counterarguments? Substantial objections. Most speeches address contingencies–different options are always available. Real objections–the ones that must be considered–include their own reasoning and support.

Anticipate audience responses.

What objections do listeners already know? Engaged listeners think along with you as you speak. They'll remember objections they've heard and more will come to them on the spot.

[1]The content of this chapter relies upon and attempts to integrate the work of the following fine texts: Edward P. J. Corbett and Rosa A. Eberly. *The Elements of Reasoning,* Allyn & Bacon, 2000; Karlyn Kohrs Campbell and Susan Schultz Huxman, *The Rhetorical Act.* Wadsworth, 2003; Rieke, Sillars, and Petersen, *Argumentation and Critical Decision Making, 6th edition.* Addison-Wesley, 2004; and Stephen Toulmin, *The Uses of Argument.* Cambridge University Press, 1995. Shortcomings in the chapter are the sole responsibility of this author.

Audience counterarguments aren't all hostile. Many are simple, inevitable questions. Work them out, don't weasel out.

- Be a Late Adopter of Technology

    1. MAIN POINT: Wait to purchase new technology if possible.

    2. ANTICIPATED AUDIENCE QUESTION: Don't cutting edge people and companies always have the latest technology? Don't you have to have the newest technology to stay ahead?

    3. PRELIMINARY ANSWER: Influential people and companies are pro-technology, but late adopters.[2]

[2]Ed Keller and Jon Berry; *The Influentials*, *Good to Great*, by Jim Collins.

Face opposing views squarely.

Engage the strongest version of an objection. Would an advocate of the counterargument affirm that you understand their position accurately?

In our mediated world, what has been called a "culture of attack" favors parties and spectators who prefer personal attacks to careful reasoning.[3] In such contexts, people who raise objections are often attacked (*ad hominem* fallacy—"attacking the person") or cartoon versions of their objections are attacked (straw man fallacy). Live audiences in the real world expect more and deserve better. Gauge a counterargument's quality in its most potent form; don't trivialize. Respond with care and offer real insight.

[3]Eric Dezenhall, *Nail 'Em! Confronting High Profile Attacks on Celebrities and Businesses*. Prometheus, 1999.

Fix flawed arguments.

Diagnose and repair defects in your message. Objections reveal gaps, errors, and weaknesses in your thinking. Counterarguments clarify what it will take to better inform or persuade your listeners, help to prioritize your reasons, and show where you need more evidence.

Identify Objections

Play "devil's advocate" with your own message. Argue from another point of view as an exercise. Aim tough questions at your message from multiple angles—including questions and objections others have not raised. Answer the following questions:

What objections have you already heard publicly?

List and outline counterarguments that are already on the table. What objections are people talking about that relate to the message?

What counterarguments have you already thought of yourself?

Note the questions and counterarguments that have come up in your own mind. Where is your message most vulnerable?

What questions does the message invite?

Think through the questions prompted by your speech. A good message generates good questions; mediocrity dulls the mind. What follow-up questions should listeners ask if they take the message seriously?

What basic assumptions ground the message?

Outline the basic beliefs that listeners need to embrace the message. What questions would someone ask from a different point of view?

What stock objections may apply?

Work through a generic list of stock questions to identify potential counterarguments. Stock questions provide different perspectives and take your mind to different places to find potential objectives.

Respond to Objections

Prepare a good faith response. Avoid the common temptation to dismiss objections. You may miss the force of a counterargument until you try to construct a good response.

Note: During the invention process, refuting a counterargument is not aimed at dissuading the audience. We are still working to strengthen the substance of our message for listeners.

Follow this process for each objection:[4]

[4]Jo Sprague and Douglas Stuart, *The Speaker's Handbook*, p. 304. Wadsworth, 2005.

State the objection.

Put the counterargument into draft form as though everything is at stake. Assume that the counterargument will prevail.

- Make the substance of the objection clear.
- Frame the objection in a way that would be acceptable to its most serious and best qualified advocates.
- Construct the objection to present the greatest challenge to your message.

State the impact of the objection.

Explain the implications of the counterargument on the issue it addresses within the message.

- The objection addresses the message in this way...
- If accurate and applicable, the objection would impact the message at this point in this way...

Address the objection.

Rebut the counterargument.

- However, the objection is mistaken and inapplicable because...
- However, the objection would be applicable, but is mistaken because...
- However, the objection would be accurate, but inapplicable because...

- The objection is accurate and applicable, but in a limited way because...
- The objection is accurate and applicable, but complementary because...

Review the impact of your rebuttal.

Discuss the implications of your response to the objection. "Therefore, the objection cannot be sustained, because..."

Deciding When to Address an Objection

Every substantial objection should be considered by a speaker, but not all should be addressed. How do you decide when to respond to a counterargument?

- Common Knowledge: Respond when the audience already knows the objection.
- Word of Mouth: Respond when the audience is likely to hear the objection after the speech.
- Self-generating: Respond when the audience may generate an objection themselves.
- Major Advantage: Respond when addressing an objection will strengthen the case, even if the audience might not know or hear the objection.

Is ignoring an objection unethical? Some say "always!" and it can be. But time does not permit every objection to be presented, so when you need to make choices, follow the guidelines above.

Question Pitfalls

Coverage vs. Problems.

No matter how well organized, covering material alone leads to monotony and distraction. Forget about covering material as your goal. The important material will get covered. Focus on how to use your material to bring the message to life for the audience. Coverage kills the material for the audience, even if it lives for the speaker.

Description vs. Challenges.

Description is not arrangement. A good narrative structure features plot and action. Description provides details, not direction. A long description provides a series of tangents and digressions leading nowhere.

Irrelevant Issues.

Questions alone will not lead to a good speech structure. To guide good arrangement, the issues must reside within the experience and expectation of the audience. Problems in the speech must resonate with listeners' own lives. Excessive questions and irrelevant questions create labyrinths of meaninglessness. So stick to the main issues.

STRUCTURE FOR LISTENERS

Organize for the ear—you're arranging the message to be heard.

The structure does important work for you. A good speech structure provides a common listening path along which the audience and speaker can think together. Therefore, good speaking structures are simple, dynamic, and flexible. Build it with care!

Arrangement—the organization process—drives the speech. When you organize, you create the context for your content. Structure the message to meet audience needs—it carries the freight. Follow audience logic; don't expect listeners to follow your personal logic. Instead, apply common structures that make your message in easy-to-follow for others.

Structure to attract listeners.

Highlight the questions that drive the message. Make the most dynamic human elements most prominent. Organize around the dramatic tension in your message—unresolved problems, paradoxes, and dilemmas.

Arrange for emphasis.

Develop the point of the speech through the structure. The central message should be clear from the organizational structure alone. Prioritize crucial ideas, themes, and support for your audience.

Organize for easy tracking.

Arrange a speech that's easy for listeners to follow. Detailed outlines distract listeners. Limit the number of speaking points. Avoid digressions, tangents, and other complications. Wander too far and you'll lose listeners.

Drive The Message With Good Arrangement

Use your organizational structure to create a pattern that helps the audience "get" the point. Put the organizational pattern to work for you and your listeners–rely on the structure to guide the remainder of the design process.

A good speaking structure helps you decide what to keep out of the speech. The point of the structure is *not* to get as much info as possible into the speech. Only say what's absolutely necessary. The structure also works to identify what your main speaking points should be and where you'll need to utilize support for those speaking points.

Choose a structure first.

A good organizational pattern puts good material you've generated into a form listeners can grasp. Connect your audience to your content by selecting a common speaking structure that fits your message to existing mental pathways in listeners. Then adapt and adjust the structure to your speech. No structure dictates your words, but a good structure will make the speech more memorable...for the listeners and the speaker.

Select from common, off-the-shelf structures.

Choose an existing (pre-fabricated) speaking structure; don't make one up on your own. "Off-the-shelf" structures make the proposition clear and give listeners the best shot at getting that point. Here's why pre-fabricated speaking structures make sense:

- Natural Patterns of Oral Thought. We use common structures to think on our feet. Remember that the audience will be thinking on their feet as they follow your message.

- Easy for Audiences to Follow. Listeners are already familiar with the logic of common speaking structures. Common structures reflect people's everyday thought patterns.

- Easy for Speakers to Remember. Common structures are already in our heads. When you create your own structure "from scratch," you're in new territory and risk losing your way.

- Mental Templates for Creativity. Common structures give simple prompts that feature the message's primary content. You're free to focus attention on sharpening the substance and support rather than fine-tuning your organizational plan.

- Enhance Delivery. Common structures create a context for confidence. You're more likely to know where you are in the speech and why every step of the way.

Keep the structure simple.

The audience needs to be able to follow your message by ear (and so do you). If you can't remember the basic structure of your speech without notes, how will the audience ever remember the message?

In conversation, we use "off-the-shelf" speaking structures all the time: someone asks a serious question and we use a simple structure that fits the kind of question we've been asked. Organize for public speaking the same way. Common speaking structures are just slightly more formal versions than what we use in conversation. Use a structure you can remember with ease. Your audience will thank you.

Common Speaking Structures

The message, the situation, and the speaker's role all contribute to the best choices of organizational structure for a speech. Select a structure, then adapt it creatively as you develop the speech.

The sample structures appear with three main points (introduction and conclusion do not count as main points). Stick with three points when possible. But when you have a good reason to vary, by all means adjust the number of points. No laws dictate the number of main points in a good speech. In practice, simplicity and audience resonance is the rule.

Problem/solution.

Messages that answer "what" questions (What ought? What not? What next? So what?). The problem-solution structure is a most useful arrangement for the workplace, where speeches so frequently take a proposal form.

	PROBLEM	SOLUTION	IMPLICATIONS	
INTRO	What's the problem?	What's the solution?	How does the solution address the problem?	CONC
	Cell phones are running people's lives.	*Create workable limits.*	*Treat cell phones like the tools they are.*	

Cause/effect (or effect/cause).

Messages that answer "why" questions. Causal reasoning, cause-and-effect is one of the most basic forms of thought we rely upon in all sorts of contexts. Note that the first two points are easily reversed (effect/cause/implications).

	CAUSE	EFFECT	IMPLICATIONS	
INTRO	Why?	What is the effect?	So what?	CONC
	Technology says "Must!"	*Cell phones are running people's lives*	*If you don't control technology, it'll control you.*	

Sequence (or time).

Messages that answer "how," "how to," and "when" questions. This speaking structure is also sometimes known as "chronological." The structure can work out of sequence as well, as long as the rationale for the shift is made clear to listeners. For example, people are quite capable of thinking in reverse order or beginning in the present, and then moving to the future, and finishing in the past.

	FIRST	SECOND	THIRD	
INTRO	How does the process or story begin?	What's the turning point?	How does it conclude? (And why does it matter?)	CONC
	You've got to have a cell phone.	*The culture invites constant use.*	*Cell phones reprioritize life and attention.*	

System (or space).

Messages that answer "where" questions and questions about relationships between persons, places, or things. This structure emphasizes how one thing is interrelated with another. In some cases system or sequence structures may work similarly. But start simple—choose one structure and stick with it initially.

	INITIAL FOCUS	RELATE & CONNECT	IMPLICATIONS	
INTRO	What draws immediate attention? (Symptom)	What's the connection to the larger system/how does the system work? (Diagnosis)	What response does it cause or call for? (Prognosis & Prescription)	CONC
	Cell phones make life safe and convenient.	*People feel social pressure to own and use cell phones.*	*Set your own terms for cell phone use.*	

Analogical.

Messages that answer "what is it like" questions. A good analogy can engage us quite forcefully. Analogical reasoning is potent. But use it with care, because it is subject to abuse. When used badly the fallacies are sometimes difficult to detect.

	ANALOGY	COMPARE	IMPLICATIONS	
INTRO	What is it like?	How do they compare?	So what?	CONC
	Cell phones are like watches—a "god on the wrist."	*Both technologies change how we think and live.*	*We need to control our use of tools or they use us.*	

Analysis/synthesis.

Messages that answer "how does it work" questions about part(s) and whole. People enjoy taking things apart and then putting them back together again. The dynamic movement of this structure can move in either direction (part/whole or whole/part).

	ANALYZE PART(S)	LOOK AT WHOLE	IMPLICATIONS	
INTRO	What parts are contributing factors?	What's the big picture?	What response does the new perspective suggest?	CONC
	Cell phones are running people's lives.	*Digital technology has radically changed personal communication.*	*We face huge new demands in personal communication.*	

Thaw/change/freeze.

Messages that answer "why change now" questions. Speeches that question the status quo or that speak to hostile audiences may use this structure to raise questions about existing positions. The crucial test is: Can the proposed alternative to the current order of things be supported?

	THAW	CHANGE	FREEZE	
INTRO	Crucial weaknesses in the existing framework?	Proposed change in existing framework?	Support from *within the audience* calls for and reinforces the proposed change?	CONC
	Cell phone slavery causes real problems.	*Revise practices and expectations for others.*	*Use cell phones to serve our purposes.*	

A family of problem/solution structures.

Workplaces are dominated by problem-solving processes and presentations. Whether you are making a sales presentation, policy proposal, or some form of recommendation, problem/solution structures will serve you well.

The basic form of problem/solution thinking requires that we identify the problem, propose a solution (or describe one already implemented), and then discuss the implications of the solution including how the solution addresses the problem and why we recommend it as the best approach.

The following list of structures presents variations on the basic problem/solution structure. The variations provide ways of utilizing this common sense structure most effectively depending on the nature of the problem and the situation in which the problem needs to be addressed.

	Intro	Point 1	Point 2	Point 3	Conc
Basic Problem-Solution		Establish problem	Propose a solution	Support with rationale	
Problem-Alternative-Solution		Establish problem	Explain 2-3 viable options	Present best option	
Problem-Cause/ Solution		Establish problem	Explain cause	Propose solution	
Monroe's Motivated Sequence	Attn Engage audience	Need Establish problem	Satisfy Propose solution	Visualize Show impact of yes-or-no proposal	Action Call for audience to take action

Add Basic Elements of Speech Arrangement

To lead listeners through the speech and focus their attention as it unfolds, use the basic elements of speech arrangement (introduction, transitions, and conclusion) to help listners focus and fill gaps they miss during the course of the speech. The basic elements do important work in the message:

Invite listeners into the speech.

Why should people listen? If you don't get the audience's attention immediately, you may never get it.

Cultivate goodwill.

Why should people listen to you? Good speakers take the goodwill of the audience seriously. When something real is at stake for listeners, goodwill becomes a condition for meaningful communication between speaker and audience.

Goodwill must be sought and earned by the speaker. Power or necessity can force people to listen to a speaker. But no speaker can demand the goodwill, respect, or trust of an audience. Great speakers cultivate goodwill from start to finish.

Hold audience interest.

Can you keep their attention? Listeners need occasional wake up calls. Use transitions to stimulate lagging listeners.

Reinforce the point.

Will they get the message? Not if you only say it once. To listen well, we need redundancy. We need to hear the main message a number of different times and different ways.

The law of primacy and recency teaches us that we remember best what we hear first and what we hear last. Although the body of the speech carries the substance of your message, a good introduction primes listeners for the point of the message. A good conclusion returns to the point deliberately and decisively. Quality messages are arranged to get the audience involved and focused on the point, not the speaker. To do their work best, the introduction and conclusion, need to be clear, concise, memorable, and tightly tied to the point of the message.

Provide closure.

What will you leave with listeners? What you say last implies, "So the conclusion of the matter really is..." What's the "take home" value of the message? Drive the content, direction, and action of the message as you close.

BASIC SPEECH ELEMENTS

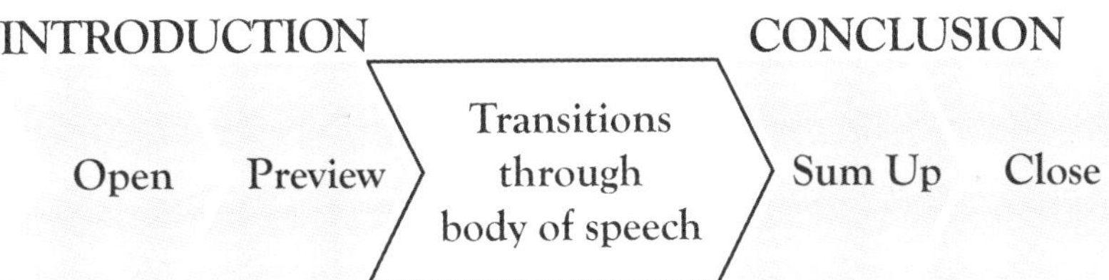

If the audience only hears your introduction, transitions, and conclusion they should still get the message!

Create Basic Elements of Arrangement

Open and close.

> *Design the first and last things you say to draw audience attention to the content of the message.* Enter and exit the speech decisively and deliberately. Avoid "snoozer losers." Perhaps thousands of speeches will be given today that begin, "Hello. My name is...and I'm here to talk to you today about..." Other "snoozer losers" (common starting phrases) to be avoided: "My topic today is..."; "The title of my speech is..."; or "They asked me to speak to you today about..."
>
> Translation: "I wish I was doing anything besides this speech. I'm not interested and have nothing of value to say. You probably won't like this speech; maybe you should go to sleep."

Always begin with a decisive attention-getter. Tie the opener to the heart of the message, even if the audience doesn't "get it" at first. After the opener, include introductions, welcomes, and acknowledgements. It's no sin to introduce yourself and the topic, just don't do it first thing!

Consider options like these:

- Story/scenario. Tell a story that connects the audience to the message, whether true, hypothetical (scenario), or fictional. Use only stories that you know well, that are brief, and that will direct attention to the heart of the message. (The shorter the speech, the shorter the story should be.)

- Question. Raise a stimulating question.

  Rely on questions with multiple answers that listeners can give. Avoid obvious questions ("how many of you have...?"), "guess my answer" questions, and rhetorical questions.

- Quotation. Relate an interesting statement from a person (familiar or famous).

  Keep it simple and know it well. A quote may come from someone directly or from a book, poem, film, or play (familiarity to the audience is key). Content is crucial–it should create an immediate connection. If it requires explanation, it's not a good attention getter.

- Fact. Cite a dramatic fact, statistic, or study.

  As openers, facts (or "factoids") must stimulate listeners, connect the audience to the message, and be simple to grasp. A pleasant surprise is as good as a shock–shock value is overrated. But obvious facts, random facts, isolated details, and good information can be deadly openers. The audience should be gripped by every opening fact(s).

Preview and summarize.

Give the audience an agenda that lets them know what to expect as the speech develops. Obviously as speakers we don't need to preview and summarize for ourselves. We already know what we're going to say, and why. But for listeners trying to grasp a message for the first time, previews and summaries do a world of good.

Let the content and structure of the message guide your preview and summary. Good ones do not draw attention to themselves. You can do this work well without much fanfare. The preview includes necessary preliminaries (thanks, acknowledgements, etc.), and tells listeners the topic and direction of the message. A summary provides a quick review of the message. You can preview and summarize in a variety of ways:

- Structure. Explain how you will move through the organizational pattern. In closing, review the territory you have covered with the audience step-by-step.

Example: "First we'll analyze the problem at some depth, then we'll look at possible approaches to the problem. Finally, I'll discuss our best option under current conditions."

- Content. Brief listeners on the ideas and issues you'll cover in the speech. To summarize, recap crucial ideas and issues by including prime sources of support, implications, and applications of the message.

  Example: "We'll be thinking through a number of issues related to this problem today, but the most important things we'll consider are...in the end, we'll have to decide the best ways to tackle this problem once and for all."

- Point. State or re-state the purpose of the speech directly and your goals in presenting it. Return at the end to reinforce the point specifically and remind listeners of your purpose in the speech.

  Example: "The heart of the problem was...and we have looked at a proposal to...because we think that...."

Transition.

Use a simple Review–Bridge–Preview format to link speaking points/ episodes. No one should notice a good transition, but it plays a vital role in the progress of the speech.

What does a good transition do if nobody notices? It resets the speech and renews audience attention. Build a brief summary of one speaking point, bridge to the next speaking point, and re-connect with listeners in the process. A simplified example of a transition in a problem-alternatives-solution speech might sound something like this:

"We've gotten a clear sense for why we should be concerned about... (review) But what are we doing about it? We have a number of options, (bridge) but only three are viable, so we'll look specifically at these three options right now...(preview)"

Don't rush to get through the transition to the next part of the speech. Let it do its work.

Refine Connections

Fashion an approach that will connect with listeners immediately, invite them into the message, and reinforce the point without drawing attention to itself. The agenda setting and managing parts of your speech arrangement are not just about process. In every case, they have a role to play in setting up and advancing the message. Therefore, build introductions, transitions, and conclusions that set a tone in the speech that resonates with the episodes and corresponds with the message as the episodes develop more fully.

- Create an Attention Getter. Give listeners a reason to listen (no gimmicks). A good attention getter draws attention to the message, not the speaker.

- Preview: Capsulize the Message. Orient the audience to how the speech will proceed.

  The preview sets the agenda for the speech. A good agenda integrates process and content. Note: It is not necessary to give the entire speech in miniature, to list the speaking episodes mechanically, or to "give away" the point of the speech. The preview sets expectations and creates anticipation, but it does not need to tell the whole story before the story has been told!

- Develop Transitions. Signal shifts from one episode to the next and re-engage listeners.

  A transition bridges two episodes or leads to the conclusion of the message. A good transition provides closure to the preceding episode, including its relevance to the larger message; refocuses the attention of the audience; and introduces the next episode. This should be accomplished with brevity and precision. A noticeable transition—one that feels like an interruption—is a failed transition. A good transition does its work seamlessly.

- Summary: Review the Message. Revisit the message and its point.

  In some cases you will revisit touchpoints along the course of the message with care. In other cases, the summary will focus on clarifying the message and the rationale behind it one last time. In every case, the summary should finalize the answer to the audience's question, "What's the point?"

- Prepare a Clean Close. Wrap up the speech with a carefully considered, decisive finish.

  Many speakers do not prepare a conclusion. They plan to figure something out when they get to the end or have only a vague, general plan for closing. In most cases they do not finish well, ending the speech awkwardly and limiting the positive impact of the message.

You Don't Know What You're Saying...

...if you cannot prepare a decisive close.

Dr. Doug Pedersen, a seasoned public speaking teacher, used to insist that speakers prepare a conclusion before planning an introduction.

"Introductions are easy," he'd say, "but lots of speakers can't get out of a speech with dignity. They don't really know what they're saying. And you have to know what you're saying to close the speech well."

You need a good exit strategy.

Whether you prepare your conclusion or introduction first, you have to have a decisive plan to reinforce the proposition of the speech and to fix it in the mind of the audience.

Non-Verbal Transitions and Conclusions

How do you signal major moves in your speech? Words are secondary.

Alert listeners to transition with non-verbal signals. They'll notice that one segment of the speech is ending and another is beginning. Pause, change your voice, slow your pace, or moderate your gestures. The non-verbal behaviors set up your transition to the next segment of the speech.

Then make the verbal move.

Words and ideas are still important, but without the non-verbal factor, listeners may miss the transition entirely. And a decisive close depends much more on non-verbals than on wording. If you neglect non-verbal signals, you could say "the end" and catch listeners completely off guard.

With basic non-verbal cues, listeners will know what you're doing when you stop speaking, no matter what you say.

Structure Pitfalls

Common speech structures:

- Start with Points, Not Structure. Don't pick out "speaking points" before you select a structure. Select a structure first, then tailor the structure to the message as you define speaking points.
- Topical Structure. Avoid "create-your-own" organization patterns. Topical structures often expect listeners to think like the speaker instead of adjusting the speaker's thinking to serve the audience. Use common structures whenever possible.
- Detailed Outlining. Don't arrange a speech as an "essay on its hind legs." Outlines are for written composition. When planning to speak, work with speaking structures to format the message for listeners instead of readers.

Introductions, transitions, and conclusions:

- No Attention Getter. Speakers introduce everything but the message. In particular, avoid introductions and other preliminaries prior to the attention getter. Such intrusions suppress audience attention and negate any supposed opener.
- Intro as Info Dump. Speakers devote too much time to the introduction. Why? Poor preparation. Often a speaker overestimates audience need for background info. A well designed intro can do its work in less than 10% of the speech.
- Review as Introduction. The first main point rehearses a prior message. This dreadful approach follows "good educational practice." Listeners hear nothing new or compelling, as if it were an invitation to go to sleep. Integrate refresher points where they apply in the context of the current message, not in the introduction.

- False Conclusions. Some speakers conclude multiple times. "As we close...in conclusion...finally...and one last point..." etc. Others end abruptly. "Thank you" is not a close. "Are there any questions?" is not a close. Prepare an exit strategy for the speech and use it!

DEVELOP EPISODES

You want a speech that's memorable for listeners, right? You want to be able to think well on your feet, right?

Speak in episodes.

In ordinary conversation, we don't speak or listen in outline or paragraph form. We speak in episodes–the basic unit of a message that matches how we think on our feet when we're talking.

Think of an episode as a self-contained "speech capsule"–a one-point mini-speech that links easily with other episodes. As a speaker, you never need to remember more than one episode at a time.

When you talk in episodes, you'll remember the speech more easily and listeners will be more likely to get the message.

Priority:

Develop the content of each speaking point in your organizational structure as an episode. Well-constructed episodes follow oral patterns that make the message come alive for listeners.

- Create the Substance of the Message Through Episodes. Transform the speaking structure into a content-rich message. Build each speaking episode using the best ideas you developed in the invention process (see Chapters 6-10).

- Design Each Episode to Serve a Purpose. Decide what you need to accomplish in each episode. Different episodes serve distinct purposes in the speech. Figure out how to make each episode do its work well for you.

- Make a Simple Case in Each Episode. Design speaking points as interlocking, one-point mini-speeches. Your goal is to make each episode strong with reasoning, evidence, and other content that meets audience needs. The episodes work together to accomplish the overall purpose of the speech.

Practical Eloquence

Do you want to be eloquent?

Speak simply, not simplistically. Make a significant, deliberate move with every speaking point—a move that advances the speech.

Your speaking structure should establish a clear pattern of related episodes, like a series of scenes in a movie. Each episode works on its own, contributes to the speech as a whole, and moves the message to your conclusion.

Together, well-developed episodes provide a coherent, substantial speech for the audience ...and you can move through the speech with ease.

EPISODIC PATTERNING

A narrator in an oral culture...normally and naturally operated in episodic patterning....We must not forget that episodic structure was the natural way to talk out a lengthy story line if only because the experience of real life is more like a string of episodes than it is like a Freytag pyramid [dramatic structure: rising action-climax-falling action]. (145)

~**Walter J. Ong,** *Orality and Literacy*

Build Speaking Points as Episodes:

Lead with content addressed to audience needs, then frame the speaking point as an episode to help listeners engage the message.

- Review Audience Questions. What audience question(s) are you answering in this episode? Give priority to addressing listener concerns that should be driving your message.

- Assemble Material. What will you need to make the speaking point? Focus on reasons, evidence, examples, and other support that belong within the particular episode you will build.

- Choose an Approach. How will you frame the speaking point as an episode? Plan your moves through the episode. Whether you make a formal argument or relate a story, you don't need an elaborate sub-structure–just a clear path to keep you on track.

- Example: *Deceits That Can Hurt–A "Pleasure Principle."*

    AUDIENCE QUESTION(S): What are some commonly-practiced forms of lying that have serious consequences?

    ASSEMBLE MATERIAL: *Sexual History–Risks of Mixed Messages.*

    Study *Sexual History* by Sunya Williams, Ph.D. in Psychology Today by Diana Burrell. Williams says that people lie extensively about their sexual history. The people who lie most often and most harmfully know the dangers to their partners and believe that their lies are unacceptable...but lie anyway. According to a National Marriage Project report (http://marriage.rutgers.edu/Publications/pubsexwostrings.htm), "Sex without Strings, Relationships without Rings," people "hooking up" expect their partners to lie about sexual history and function on a "trust no one" principle.

    APPROACH TO THE EPISODE: The ideas and material can be presented in a worst-case/best-case scenario adapted to the particular audience. The goal of the episode will be to explain a range of practical implications concerning short-term and long-term risks tied to the lies.

Refine Episodes:

Customize the message within a form that fits the message and that incorporates timely reasons, support, and connections for the audience.

- Think of the Episode as a Short Story. What kind of human action, decisions, or challenges are involved in the speaking point?

  The episode should be coherent. What do you need the audience to hear and do through this particular speaking point? You might not tell a single actual story in the whole speech, but you do want every speaking point to answer the question, "What's the story with this episode?"

- Give Reasons. Every major argument for the message must appear in one of your speaking episodes.

  Episodes are the place in which you do your most careful reasoning. Not every episode will include a formal argument, but every episode must contribute in some way to the larger case or argument of the message.

- Provide Support. Incorporate all of you supporting material through speaking episodes.

  Establish, reinforce, document, and validate your message through evidence and other support. Weave the support for your message into your episodes. Refer to evidence and other forms of support clearly where appropriate.

- Refute Objections. Address primary concerns, challenges, and counter-arguments within speaking episodes.

  You may dedicate one speaking point to answer objections, or you may deal with challenges as they emerge through the course of the message.

- Connect with the Audience. Adapt each episode to the reasoning patterns, expectations, and experience of listeners.

  To engage the audience requires thorough adaptation from start to finish. Meet the audience in every point on their own terms (see Chapter 15).

Meaning in Speech Depends on Context

The content of a message is only relevant, meaningful, and memorable in context.

Low context forms (e.g. data points, bullet points, and statistical reports) ask audiences to do the work of supplying context. Many audiences check out and maintain a polite façade in response.

Many speakers mistake abstract content as the "real message" and think of putting the content into the audience contexts as an unwelcome difficulty. They might even consider putting the message in context as "dumbing down" the content.

The very things that could help the audience understand the message most are considered to be obstacles!

High context forms (e.g. stories, parables, dialogue, and scenarios) literally bring life to content and therefore bring the message to the life of the audience.

Context carries content.

- Low Context: Binge drinking is a huge problem on college campuses today. (This is true, but gives the impression that most students are binge drinkers.)
- High Context: For most, binge drinking is not a problem. New college students tend to binge drink once or twice, then stop. They see the dangers with a brief encounter. Binge drinking is a big problem, but it involves a small proportion that don't quit.

Prepare a Flowchart (Not an Outline)

A speech is a lot more like a film or a play than a written essay.

Filmmakers and stage directors plot the action and dialogue of a film frame-by-frame, and scene-by-scene to integrate the thinking, motives, and actions of each character. A flowchart can help you do the same as you arrange your speech. Flowcharts keep your attention focused on the major action and conversation of the speech—your moves, themes, and ideas.

Many books, teachers, and speakers say to organize speeches by outlining the message as you would a composition (including writing the speech as a text, word for word).

Outlines work well for written composition, but they tempt us to obsess about details and wording. This is important for good writing, but distracting for good speaking.

When you arrange your message, don't start with words and details the audience will never remember. Start with a flowchart!

Detail-mania: Enough is Enough!

Speakers have been boring audiences with unnecessary, forgettable details for thousands of years.

People need just enough detail to get the point. If listeners can get the point with a single example, never use two! If listeners can get the point with two examples, never use three!

For listeners, details create an exquisite monotony. Most tangents, digressions, and details please only the speaker. Build your speaking episodes only on your best material, your best sources, your best stories, your best examples, and your best evidence.

Audiences don't even remember most details, so drop them and keep the message moving.

Episode Pitfalls

- Conditions and Qualifications. Give only essential context; err on the side of brevity.

  Speakers who "over-contextualize" with too many conditions, too many qualifications, and too much background cloak the message. Keep the speaking point in the audience's view—no distractions!

- Over-structuring. Too much structure obscures the content. If you let the bones of the message stick out, the speech becomes grotesque. Make speaking structures simple with a clear point and a clear connection to the message in each episode.

- Uniform Approach. Formulaic mechanisms bore audiences. Variety is the spice of life. Use different patterns for each episode and don't speak like a droid. Speech design is a practical, creative art, not a technique.

EPISODE STRUCTURING EXERCISE

Basic format.

In this set of exercises, speakers present abridged versions of a longer message that focuses on elements of arrangement.

The speaker needs to comfortably present basic elements of speech structure without notes (notes will be used to support details, not organizational patterns).

Purpose.

To learn and practice arrangement of spoken messages that speakers and listeners can both remember.

To follow the message, listeners need a clear pattern of organization. A fitting structure for the body of the message, supported by a well-designed introduction, transitions, and conclusion, provide a much better chance of memorability. Reliance on stock structures and patterns actually frees students to speak more creatively and energetically with better content getting to listeners.

Activities.

The short speech exercises suggested below require selection of a simple point and two reasons with support. Use a three-minute time limit. For all three speeches:

- Use the topical invention system to find seven possible reasons. Pick two.
- For the selected reasons, find two different forms of backing for each one.

Based on the work above, prepare a three-minute, one-point speech on one of the following topics:

1. We should all learn...

   Fill in the blank with something that you think you and your listeners need to learn that would benefit them and people close to them (e.g. a specific skill, a particular foreign language, a trade, specific knowledge, etc.).

2. A great, uncommon gift to give that can't be bought...

   Fill in the blank with a gift that listeners can/should give that cannot be bought with money. The gift needs to be commonly available, but uncommonly given.

3. We need to change... even though you won't hear about it on the Internet or TV.

   Fill in the blank with something that you think needs to change, but that is not typically in the popular mindset, whether in the news media, popular culture, or as a common topic in school/work, (e.g. how we think about children; eating alone; worrying about "–isms"; grading by eliminating, etc.).

Speak Their Language 5

Tuning the Message

"...in oratory the very cardinal sin is to depart from the language of everyday life, and the usage approved by the sense of the community."

–Cicero, *de Oratore*, **I.iii.12**

"What profits correctness in a speech which is not followed by the listeners when there is no reason for speaking if what is said is not understood by those on whose account we speak?

"This principle is valid not only in conversations whether with one person or with several, *but it is to be insisted upon much more when [speeches] are delivered to the people so that we may be understood."*

–Augustine, *de Doctrina Christiana*, **IV.24-25**

How to Talk, Not What Words to Say

For public speaking, the question of language is "how to talk?" with the audience about the message, not what specific words you will use.

When you're composing written sentences, you try to find just the right word. Good writers are always revising and editing, trying out different words in different combinations until it feels right.

Speaking well demands thinking on your feet. You don't write out the words to get them right. You think through the kind of language that the message and audience will require. Yes, you may select key terms or phrases that you will need to rely on in the speech as key ideas that you want to use in a certain way.

Focus on the language of conversation, not the language of composition.

PURPOSE: *To use language that makes the content understandable and engaging for listeners.*

PRINCIPLE: *The spoken word requires us to converse in language within the audience's usage.*

PRACTICE: *Oral translation exercises.*

LOCATE THE LANGUAGE

When was the last time you learned something new when you didn't understand the language?

Our most dramatic insights and greatest advances take place when people who are speaking in ordinary language help us to see things in extraordinary ways.

Perhaps more important, all the fun in speech lives within ordinary language. Jokes, irony, slang, and satire are all ordinary language forms put to extraordinary uses. Creativity, learning, and fun all reside within ordinary language—the most interesting language!

Unfamiliar language stifles communication no matter what you think about what you said or how well you said it. If we miss ordinary language, either we don't know the audience or we don't really know the message...or both. Therefore, always work within the ordinary language of the audience. You meet the audience and communicate best in common speech.

Focus on content.

Ordinary language provides the best access to content. Grasping meaning in the message depends on context; ordinary language provides the highest degree of context.

Avoid confusion.

Unfamiliar language muddles the message. Listeners struggle when speakers work outside ordinary language. You'll distract people with constant digressions to define terms and concepts.

Create connections.

Listeners engage new ideas well within ordinary language. Listeners can gain knowledge, insight, and wisdom through speeches grounded in ordinary language. Speakers can connect with audiences to introduce ideas through new combinations and contexts within familiar languages.

Vernaculars

Speak in the vernacular—the common tongue of the whole audience.

The vernacular is the ordinary language of listeners in our present moment. Vernacular language is the standard of every person and culture's common fluency in speech.

The audience defines what qualifies as vernacular. If you're speaking to an audience of world-class chemists about their work, the vernacular is not the "language of the street," it's the research language of the laboratory.

If you seek to communicate with the entire audience, the vernacular is essential. Only when you intend to exclude, dismiss, disregard, or target should you depart from the vernacular to use jargon or "high-brow" language, vocabulary, and grammar.

Working with Language in the Speech

Find the language intersection between the message, listeners and speakers. The goal is to raise the message to the highest common denominator. You'll speak best when you're presenting the most complex message the audience can consider. The prime issue for speaker is how the language sounds to the audience.

For example an audience with specialized knowledge requires a highly specialized language; to simplify would be an error. An audience with a wider spectrum of members demands a more basic, widely-shared language. But even with large audiences, good speakers push audience limits of complexity.

Work toward speaking the audience's ordinary language in the richest sense possible.

Question your assumptions.

> *What am I taking for granted that this audience might not take for granted?* Don't assume that the audience's language matches yours. Review your language and check whether you are counting on shared meanings that may not, in fact, be shared by your audience. Take the message to the audience in their language, don't try to bring them into yours.

Find the audience's language.

What language(s) does the audience live in? What people talk about and how they talk about it varies from time to time and place to place. One way to learn the audience's language is to find out what words, voices, and images dominate their lives at work, at home, in the media, and in their communities.

What are they talking about and to whom? What are they listening to, reading, and watching? What are they speaking and writing about? How do they talk to themselves?

Fit the message within language.

What are the best points of entry to the message for listeners? Put each speaking point into the audience's language. Where does the language of the audience resonate best with each part of the speech? Find good starting points in familiar language so the audience can get into the speech.

Translate key terms, themes, and ideas.

How can I say it in their language? Some ideas and segments of the message may not fit easily within ordinary language for listeners. Translation for speech involves more than words. Language forms and patterns work together with vocabulary to make the message come alive for the audience.

Look for trouble spots.

Where are language difficulties most likely to occur in the message for this audience? When you find complex content areas, take care with language. The trouble spots you feel are often crucial to the message, and come at points where new ideas, insights, or implications enter the speech.

Trust your intuition. If you feel like there's a problem, there probably is one.

Work with listener's terms and patterns.

What language will help the audience hear the message best? Listeners will be hearing, not reading, your speech. Think about how you would discuss the message with them informally. The language you want is much closer to a planned conversation than it is to a written essay or letter.

Code Switching

You change languages all the time. Communication scholars call this skill "code switching." Code switching means moving from one language or dialect to another fluently. We switch codes between work or school and home. We use one code with close friends and another with family.

The point is we already adapt and adjust our language in different speaking contexts based on who's listening. In public speaking, we have to do the same thing. A good communicator makes such adjustments in an authentic way.

How to Refine Language:

Ordinary language is the language that seems ordinary to the audience. Practical wisdom, knowledge, and common sense all reside within the ordinary language of a given audience.

Contemporary.

What language are listeners using today? When you're a member of the group you're speaking to, answering the question is pretty simple. As you speak to outside audiences, the question becomes more difficult and more important.

Comfortable.

What kind of language best "fits" the message to the audience? In a good message, the language doesn't draw attention to itself, distract the audience, or disrupt the audience's train of thought. A message may be complex and demanding, but good use of language never makes listeners feel left out.

Conversational.

What patterns do listeners use in ordinary conversation? There are casual and formal conversations, but all rely on oral patterns of speaking and listening.

Novels approximate many different types of speech used in ordinary conversation.[1] A speech transfers your conversational skills from personal conversation to group presentation.

[1]Mikhail Bakhtin, *Discourse in the Novel* and *Speech Genres and Other Late Essays.*

Spoken grammar is different. It's not about complete sentences and it cannot be diagrammed. The unit of speech is an utterance, not a sentence. Speeches have different rules that are tuned to ears, not to grammar books.

If You Can't Explain It, You Don't Know It

From "Before We Can Communicate" by C.S. Lewis.[2]

[2]C.S. Lewis, "Before We Can Communicate"

> What we want to see in every...exam is a compulsory paper on (simply) translation; a passage from some ...[technical or scholarly] work to be turned into plain vernacular English...
>
> You will find at once that this labour has two useful byproducts.
>
> 1. In the very process of eliminating from your matter all that is technical, learned, or allusive, you will discover, perhaps for the first time, the true value of learned language: namely, brevity. It can say in ten words what popular speech can hardly get into a hundred. Your popularisation of the passage set will have to be very much longer than the original. And this we must just put up with.
>
> 2. You will also discover—at least I, a copious 'translater', think I have discovered—just how much you yourself, up to that moment, have been understanding the language which you are now trying to translate. Again and again I have been most usefully humiliated in this way. One holds, or thinks one holds, a particular view.... And you can go on for years discussing and defending it to others *of your own sort...*
>
> ...All seems well. Then turn and try to expound this same view to an intelligent mechanic or a sincerely inquisitive, but superficially quite

irreverent, schoolboy. Some question of shattering crudity (it would never be asked in learned circles) will be shot at you....The crude question turns out to be fatal. You have never, it now appears, really understood what you have so long maintained. You haven't really thought it out; not to the end; not to the 'absolute ruddy end'.

You must either give it up, or else begin all over again. *If, given patience and ordinary skill, you cannot explain a thing to any sensible person whatever (provided he will listen), then you don't really understand it yourself.*

Language Pitfalls

Speaker jargon.

Don't mistake your ordinary language for the ordinary language of the audience. Don't expect the audience to share fluency in areas of expertise. When you speak your own language, it's easy to sound proud, phony, or foolish, and it doesn't help listeners get the message.

Superficial speech.

Ordinary language doesn't make a message shallow. When you mistake simple for simplistic you "dumb-down" a message. You risk either insulting or boring your audience. Invite the audience into the message through common language without pretense.

Inauthentic tone.

You don't need to sound like the audience to speak their language. Extend yourself toward the audience to meet them in language patterns that you can both share. Don't try to match their accents or manners of speech. The speech must communicate in the world of the audience, therefore you have to work within the common language of that world.

MNEMONIC DEVICES

Mnemonics help the audience hear the most important elements of form (organization) and content (proposition). Good mnemonics also help us gain command of the message and free us to think better as we speak. We are released from reliance on extensive notes or memorization. We can think on our feet.

To work most effectively, we must use mnemonic devices sparingly. Overuse will kill their effect. The point of mnemonics is not to remember everything, but to remember everything that is important.

Sound.

Mark your speaking points with the same beginning or ending sound. Give your listeners clear signals to follow and remember key segments and transitions in the speech.

- Same Beginning Sound

    1. *Walk* away from pseudo-familiarity.
    2. *Work* from a safe distance.
    3. *Watch* for real signs of trust to grow.

- Same Ending Sound

    1. Beware of infatua*tion.*
    2. Start with a relational cu*shion.*
    3. Base trust on real confirma*tion.*

Spoken rhythm.

Make your best ideas easy on the ears. Revise your proposition and one or two key phrases until they're simply "sayable".

Good spoken rhythm in a phrase does not draw attention to itself; it draws attention to the content. Bad rhythm or lack of rhythm gets in the way of the most important ideas.

- Good Spoken Rhythm: The things that you own end up owning you.

- Bad Spoken Rhythm: You become possessed by the stuff you buy.

- No Rhythm: People buy many possessions and think that the things they buy are their own property, but really the people end up being like the things they buy.

Turns of phrase (figures and tropes).

Play with language at key points to capture listening ears. Figures of speech and thought are "high-context" memory devices. To meet the audience, turns of phrase must work within the audience's cultural knowledge and rely on terms familiar in listener experience.

Turns of phrase involve spoken rhythm, but they include more specific memory tactics as well.

- Antithesis. You contrast one idea to an opposing idea. Simple form: "Not this, but that."

- Understatement and Overstatement. You mark the importance of an idea by disrupting expected intensity.

    1. ***Understatements*** treat major issues as minor ones. The speaker points to weightiness by treating something lightly.

    2. ***Overstatements***, sometimes called *hyperboles*, exaggerate for emphasis. The speaker embellishes and amplifies.

- Irony. In its simplest form, you say exactly the opposite of what you mean. You can also speak ironically when you say what is not precisely opposite, but clearly different from what you mean as the audience understands you.

- Metaphor. Perhaps the best-known turns of phrase belong in the metaphor family. Metaphor, simile, analogy, metonymy, and synecdoche are all forms of comparison (see end of chapter).

Intonation.

Voice inflection is as important as word choice. For speakers and listeners, memory depends heavily on how you speak, not just on what you say. Therefore, every mnemonic device and every turn of phrase–everything you want the audience to remember most–has to be really sayable by you.

Work ideas and phrases into easy to say rhythms and inflections for your voice. It has to work for you. When you remember sayings, lines, and phrases, you always remember them with the intonations that you've heard or added.

Yoda and Yogi: Memorable Language

The words of Yoda, the Jedi master from *Star Wars*, and Yogi Berra, retired New York Yankees player and manager, enjoy instant recognition. Why? Trademarked figures of speech make their words memorable.

YODA: The Jedi master uses a figure of speech called hyperbaton, which is an inversion of normal word order.

- "Ready are you? What know you of ready? For eight hundred years have I trained Jedi. My own counsel will I keep on who is to be trained...This one a long time have I watched. All his life has he looked away... to the future, to the horizon. Never his mind on where he was. Hmm? What he was doing. Hmph. Adventure. Heh. Excitement. Heh. A Jedi craves not these things."
- "Try not. Do or do not... there is no try."
- "Named must your fear be, before banish it you can."

YOGI: The New York Yankee legend used a figure of speech known as acryologia or malapropism–a misapplied word. Yogi often used the same word (or its synonym) twice, once well applied and once misapplied. Yogi's version now has a unique name; it's called a "yogiism."[3]

- "It ain't over 'til it's over."
- "When you get to a fork in the road, take it."
- "You can observe a lot by watching."

[3]Jay Heinrichs calls this the "idiot savant figure." He writes a web page and has published a book on figures of speech in practice, *Thank You for Arguing: What Aristotle, Lincoln, and Homer Simpson Can Teach Us about the Art of Persuasion.*

- "It's like deja-vu, all over again."
- "Nobody goes there anymore. It's too crowded."
- "Half the lies they tell about me aren't true."

Mnemonic Pitfalls

Sentences.

Don't memorize full sentences. Learn phrase-length "sayables." Resist all rote memorization. Mnemonics are memory aids for key words and phrases.

Too simplistic.

Avoid clunky mnemonics. They need to feel right and strengthen the message without calling attention to themselves. Less is more; overuse distracts from the message.

Phony.

Don't get too cute. Never use a turn of phrase or form of repetition for its own sake. Mnemonics should make the message memorable, not the device itself.

WORD PICTURES

Imagination can take us beyond words. In a speech, listeners are moved beyond words by words that invoke images and emotions. Imagination, energized by word pictures in a speech, links listeners' hearts and minds to get them initially involved in the message and to remember more of the message for a longer period of time.

As listeners, we respond best to things we can see and hear in our minds. We call things that move us "unimaginable" because we can't fully fathom what we really are imagining.

It might seem like we're moving beyond reason when reason and emotion (heart and mind) are in play. At least we're trying to think things through.

Most people need such combinations of reason and emotion to remember and to respond in meaningful ways.

A word picture is a catalyst for imagination. Word pictures invite listeners into the scene.

For example, you could say, "The man had a dog who did tricks. He was a remarkable dog. The dog could sing."

Or you could say, "The old man had a big old dog called Watson. And what a dog he was! Like a Bernese Mountain Dog in his coat—black top coat, brown legs, big white chest, big black and brown head. But taller, longer, and lighter than a Berner, shaped more like an Afghan Hound—and not more than 80 pounds. Lanky. Yup, Watson was a purebred mutt—a rescue dog who had been abused, nobody knows how, except it was by a man. When he first came home, he shied and cowered when the old man moved fast or raised his voice. But he soon grew to love that old man...he loved everyone...and he listened. And he could sing when the music moved him—he could howl along pretty close to any French horn or cello playing on the stereo. Not perfect pitch, but close. He'd just lie on the living room floor and raise up his head and sing! Remarkable dog!"

You meet the audience with familiar language to develop a mental illustration. Word pictures in the speech encourage listeners to participate in the message, and participants remember your point.

Activate the mind.

> *Put listeners' brains in gear with word pictures.* Illustrations that we generate through language draw on mental models and can stimulate vivid, dynamic images co-created between the speaker and listener.

Internalize the message.

> *Prompt the audience to experience the message from the inside out.* Because images reside in the mind of the listener, a word picture develops internally and belongs to the listener and speaker together.

Store ideas through images.

> *Relate the message in a memorable format, one that enhances retention and recall.* Word pictures rely on our ability to store images and diagrams in our heads to later reproduce a relatively accurate version.

An effective word picture can remain in the memory of a listener much longer and more vividly than a mere string of words. The word picture can carry a wealth of embedded knowledge, well beyond mere information points, including reason, emotion, and context.

VISUAL SPEAKING
A great impression is made by dwelling on a single point, and also by clear explanation and almost visual presentation of events as if practically going on.
~Cicero, *De oratore***, Book III, Chapter LIII.202**

How to Engage Imagination

Imagination is animated by words. Speech causes memories to come alive in the present through the things we hear, the things we say to ourselves, and the things we say to others.

Visualization.

> *Imagination is driven by being able to see things in our mind's eye.* To capture imaginations, listeners must be able to envision a scene from the words. You envision the image and then put it into words.

Dynamism.

> *The best word pictures involve action.* Sheer description in a speech puts people to sleep. Put the message in an active context either in the present, in anticipation of action, or in recollection of action.

Tension.

What's at stake in the illustration? Some form of dramatic tension emerges to call for a speech. Listeners need the tension in a word picture, whether from conflict, ignorance, anticipation, desire, or another source. A good word picture reflects or intensifies the tension.

PICTURES IN OUR HEADS

We shall assume that what each man does is based not on direct and certain knowledge, but on pictures made by himself or given to him... The way in which the world is imagined determines at any particular moment what men will do.

–Walter Lippmann

Crafting Word Pictures

Speak within the commonplaces—mental images, actions, and experiences shared by the audience. Provide contours and context in action that listeners complete using their own imagination, not wordy, detailed descriptions.

Proposition and key ideas.

Don't waste word pictures on details. Place illustrations strategically. Take care to strengthen the proposition and supporting ideas to make them meaningful and memorable.

Illustrate action and tension.

What decisions must be made, consequences considered, and actions explained? Not only should word pictures illustrate action (see "Dynamism" prior), but they should point to tensions the audience is facing and decisions that ought to be made in light of the speech.

Visualize in words.

> *What in the world would this message look like in action?* Fit the word pictures into the present world, experience, and way of life for the audience. To work well, a good speech illustration must find its details in the audience's world, both in concrete details and common sensibilities.

Visualization in the Motivated Sequence

What motivates listeners to engage a message, understand it, and take appropriate action?

Alan H. Monroe developed a persuasive speaking structure (see chapter 4) to help speakers design strong motivational messages.[4] Within Monroe's five-step structure (attention, need, satisfaction, visualization, action) visualization is pivotal.

[4]*Principles and Types of Speech*, by Alan H. Monroe.

Monroe's insight realized the impact of helping audiences to see, or visualize, the potential consequences of adopting or rejecting a proposal presented in a speech.

To visualize in a speech means to create word pictures. Audiences can't see anything without them!

An Ethic of Word Pictures: To Engage, Not Distract

Word pictures spur audience imagination. But imagination can work with reason or against it. It's not an automatic plus.

Sir Francis Bacon defined rhetoric as, "The application of reason to imagination for the better moving of the will."[5] He asks a crucial question: Will imagination advance reason, or suppress it?

[5]*The Advancement of Learning*, by Francis Bacon

Bacon knows that speakers can effectively deceive by suppressing reason and distracting people with false images. To speak ethically, you've got to use word pictures to make truthful content and good ideas more vivid and memorable.

From "What to the Slave is the Fourth of July?" by Frederick Douglass

The following is an excerpt from the text of Frederick Douglass's speech presented to the Rochester Ladies' Anti-Slavery Society on July 5, 1852.[6]

[6]The full text of the speech is available at: http://www.teachingamericanhistory.org/library/index.asp?document=162.

> Mark the sad procession, as it moves wearily along, and the inhuman wretch who drives them. Hear his savage yells and his blood-chilling oaths, as he hurries on his affrighted captives! There, see the old man, with locks thinned and gray. Cast one glance, if you please, upon that young mother, whose shoulders are bare to the scorching sun, her briny tears falling on the brow of the babe in her arms. See, too, that girl of thirteen, weeping, yes! weeping, as she thinks of the mother from whom she has been torn! The drove moves tardily. Heat and sorrow have nearly consumed their strength; suddenly you hear a quick snap, like the discharge of a rifle; the fetters clank, and the chain rattles simultaneously; your ears are saluted with a scream, that seems to have torn its way to the center of your soul! The crack you heard, was the sound of the slave-whip; the scream you heard, was from the woman you saw with the babe. Her speed had faltered under the weight of her child and her chains! that gash on her shoulder tells her to move on. Follow the drove to New Orleans. Attend the auction; see men examined like horses; see the forms of women rudely and brutally exposed to the shocking gaze of American slave-buyers. See this drove sold and separated forever; and never forget the deep, sad sobs that arose from that scattered multitude. Tell me citizens, WHERE, under the sun, you can witness a spectacle more fiendish and shocking. Yet this is but a glance at the American slave-trade, as it exists, at this moment, in the ruling part of the United States.

Word Picture Pitfalls

- Overuse. The power of word pictures can become intoxicating. Audiences respond, sometimes dramatically, to skillfully developed illustrations. The antidote? Moderate and keep your focus on the content of the message, not audience effects.

- Off Target. A particular illustration misses the point or misses the audience. No illustration is good in its own right. It has to connect the message through the speaker to the audience. A good word picture in a message to one audience might flop in a similar message given to different listeners.

- Inappropriate Pictures. Word pictures can become too graphic in a variety of ways. Distress caused by inappropriate use of word pictures is rarely justifiable.

  The power of a strong but wrong word picture is difficult for listeners to resist and difficult for them to forget. Avoid verbal violence!

METAPHORS

What is a metaphor? In simple terms, a metaphor takes two or more familiar terms or ideas and puts them together in a new way. The interaction between the two ideas generates new insights, new perspectives, or new connections.

Metaphors connect reason and imagination in language. When listeners understand a metaphor, reason and imagination are working together with emotion. A metaphor such as "beer is a brawler" demonstrates how reason, imagination, and emotion interact in metaphor. Audiences are much more likely to remember a good metaphor (and so are you).

Link audience experience to ideas.

Metaphors announce new ideas where people live. Strange words do not good metaphors make. Metaphors work within the common language of the audience. The best metaphors provoke thought by placing familiar coordinates in unfamiliar, but understandable combinations.

Stimulate thinking.

Metaphors intrigue and involve the audience. When understanding a metaphor, listeners are inclined to think with a speaker rather than just hear words. Paying attention usually involves thinking on a variety of levels at the same time. Metaphors enhance audience focus by prompting listeners to incorporate their own thoughts and synchronize them with the message.

Signal priorities.

Good metaphors elevate the point of the speech. Highlight the main point of the message and clarify crucial ideas that support the point.

METAPHORS WE LIVE BY

"The reason we have focused so much on metaphor is that it unites reason and imagination." (93)

~George Lakoff and Mark Johnson

How to Find Good Metaphors

Express key ideas beginning with audience experience. Good metaphors start with the audience to cultivate new meanings.

Explore connections between the message and the audience's common sense, such as shared experiences and expectations. What is most familiar to listeners that can help them understand the ideas that propel your message? Don't use a baseball metaphor with an audience that is passionate about ballet. Ask basic questions to find good metaphors:

What's it like?

Make strategic comparisons and contrasts. We learn much by association. Metaphors brand important associations into the audience's mind to establish mental connections that move an idea into the audience's world. Ask the "what is it like?" question about the proposition of the message and other key ideas to make metaphorical associations.

What needs to be made familiar?

Create a metaphor to bridge unfamiliar ideas with the audience's frame of reference. Some of your ideas may sound strange initially to listeners. Metaphors can help you say, "You already know this, you just don't realize it yet." Merging familiar terms in unfamiliar ways spurs thinking.

What needs to be made strange?

> *Reframe an audience's assumption via metaphorical disruption.* When you want an audience to be able to see things in a different way, metaphors can deliver new perspectives on familiar territory.

Metaphors invite new insights by joining ideas that seem to conflict. Kenneth Burke, rhetorical theorist and literary critic, called this aspect of metaphor "perspective by incongruity." As Thomas S. Kuhn noted in his groundbreaking discussion of scientific revolutions, new paradigms of thought come from new metaphors as new ideas combine familiar terms in new ways.[8] To challenge conventional wisdom, you have to work within the audience's common sense, both coming and going.

[7]Kenneth Burke, *Permanence and Change.*.

[8]Thomas Kuhn *The Structure of Scientific Revolutions.*

A Metaphor Is Worth a Thousand Pictures[9]

[9]Daniel Pink, *A Whole New Mind.*

If a picture is worth a thousand words, then why not substitute pictures for words in every case?

The simple answer is that words and pictures cannot be divided as easily as the cliché suggests. A picture is only worth a thousand words if we know the words and can apply them to the picture.

On the other hand, metaphors are so powerful that some have suggested that a metaphor is worth a thousand pictures. Why? Because as Cicero noted over two-thousand years ago, "Metaphors drawn from the sense of sight are much more vivid, virtually placing within the range of our mental vision objects not actually visible to our sight."[10]

[10]*De oratore*, Book III, Chapter XXIX.160

Through metaphors, ordinary humans can spontaneously generate myriads of mental images—full-color, 3-D, moving pictures with multiple perspectives and surround sound. No matter how complex the artistic or manufactured images we design, they can't match the human imagination at work. Metaphors are one way to bring thousands of images and words into the message in ways we could never display or express.

METAPHORS WE LIVE BY

"The essence of metaphor is understanding and experiencing one kind of thing in terms of another."

~George Lakoff and Mark Johnson

How to Use Metaphors Well

Consider developing a metaphorical approach to crucial aspects of your speech.

Listeners would often like more illustrations. What do they mean? They want exactly what a good metaphor provides–words that connect to what listeners know in their lives.

For instance, what does it mean to be "good, not nice?" Good, not nice is being a good doctor, not a diet plan infomercial. Can you hear a doctor saying that there's no magic formula for weight loss? The doc looks us straight in the eye and says, "You have to eat better, eat less, and exercise more...for the rest of your life!" That's good, but it's not nice.

Metaphors are one way to help the audience visualize what a message means personally. Here are some basic types of metaphor that will enhance audience understanding and memory.

Proposition metaphors.

Find a metaphor to highlight the idea that summarizes the purpose of the message. A good metaphor makes the proposition more than a statement; it signals direction and intensity in the speech.

Neil Postman's idea in his namesake book, *Technopoly*, makes the metaphorical point that we live in a "technology monopoly." This is a system in which technology has a monopoly on the taken-for-granted way most people think and behave.

Insight metaphors.

Find a metaphor to give listeners insight into a critical idea, theme, or example. Two or three ideas in the message are essential to establishing the main proposition. Metaphors will engage listeners at turning points in the speech.

Many management gurus use animal metaphors to give audiences a hook on which to hang their ideas. Jim Collins, author of *Good to Great*, asks this question: "Is your organization a *hedgehog or a fox?*" A hedgehog survives by sticking to its core identity and principles in changing circumstances. A fox survives by always adapting, and letting circumstances control its identity.

Difficult idea metaphors.

Find a metaphor to relate complex ideas that may be difficult to explain. Metaphors are indispensable when you have complicated material to explain. What can never be completely described can often be grasped metaphorically.

Quantum chemists and physicists rely almost entirely on metaphors to explain time and space. Metaphors such as "black holes," "worm holes," and "string theory" help us think about incredibly complex ideas.

THE PLEASURE OF METAPHOR

Even in cases where there are plenty of specific words available, metaphorical terms give people much more pleasure, if the metaphor is a good one...It is a mark of cleverness of a kind to jump over things that are obvious and choose other things that are far-fetched; or because the hearer's thoughts are led to something else and yet without going astray, which is a very great pleasure.

--Cicero, *De oratore*, **Book III, Chapter XXIX.160**

The Metaphor Family

METAPHOR: X is Y	"Marriage is adoption."
SIMILE: X is like Y	"Marriage is like adoption."
ANALOGY: A metaphor or simile explained or developed at some length.	"Think of marriage as a form of adoption." When two people decide to get married, it's more than making dating or cohabitation permanent. A couple enters into a different relationship altogether. Think of marriage as a form of mutual adoption. Both are family relationships sealed with lifetime legal bonds. Both are bonds that introduce new rights, privileges, and duties for both parties. Both bond people to a common future as long as they live. Affection alone isn't enough. Adoption agencies work hard to project what the life of the new family might be like economically, relationally, religiously, and more. The adoption agency conducts a home study and learns about ordinary patterns of life in the family and how things work in the household. The agency has to be convinced that the child and adoptive family will be a good fit. Adoption is driven by the affection of prospective parents. It's a deliberate process. If the adoption occurs, the child becomes a legal member of the family forever.
IRONY: X is not Y by saying the opposite	"Marriage is trivial." Couples considering marriage shouldn't take the whole thing too seriously. They should just get married and take their chances. There's no good way to anticipate whether a marriage will last. Statistics don't lie. Stats say that marriage is a 50/50 proposition for everyone who gets married, that's the truth. It's a gamble, but why not just risk it? To overthink marriage is unromantic. Think it through and you'll kill romance. Physical attraction, desire, and affection are all that matter. Take the leap. Tie the knot. If it wasn't meant to be, you'll be in the half that didn't make it. But being realistic, you know that's a possibility going in, so you haven't lost anything.

Metaphor Pitfalls

Mere ornamentation.

Don't use metaphors as window dressing. Metaphors are sometimes associated with an ornamental use of language. In public speaking, metaphors do important cognitive work for speakers and listeners, as well as important content work in the message.

Mere cleverness.

Don't use metaphors to sound smart. Smartness is speaking about things that matter without drawing attention to oneself. Hard work to connect with listeners may result in a clever metaphor. We're rarely as clever as we think we are when cleverness is our goal.

Mere word play.

Don't use metaphors to amuse yourself. Metaphors, like other figures of thought and speech, can be fun. The priority of metaphors should be to connect with listeners, not to entertain the speaker.

SPEAK THEIR LANGUAGE EXERCISES

Basic format.

In this set of exercises, speakers present messages that focus on different types of work to meet the audience in their language.

Speakers try to help the audience get the message by using deliberate language to move the message into the world of a specific set of listeners.

Purpose.

To get a feel for how aligning examples, illustrations, and language to a specific message and audience makes speaking more dynamic and enjoyable.

Speakers have to activate oral patterns of thought in speech. The patterns that capture the imagination of listeners happen in their language.

Activities.

The short speech exercises suggested below allow speakers to practice locating messages in the language of the audience. The exercises should be done WITHOUT NOTES.

1. Kindergarten Impromptus.

   Generate a list of questions five-year-olds might ask about life. Each speaker selects a random question and has one minute to provide a truthful answer in language that would help a five-year-old understand without feeling "talked down to."

2. Major Metaphor Groups ("What's It Like?" Speeches).

   Provide a series of topics about basic problems with health, travel, government, school, exercise, money, etc. Each speaker selects a topic and takes three to five minutes to pick a metaphor group to use for a one-minute speech explaining the problem and/or solution (e.g. sports metaphors, music metaphors, building metaphors, cooking metaphors, medical metaphors, vehicle metaphors, battle metaphors, etc.).

3. Visualization: Best Case/Worst-Case Scenarios.

   Use a speech you are preparing for presentation. If necessary, turn the message into a specific proposal. (Alternative: Use a list of random, fun proposals.) Give a one- to two-minute presentation that gives a best-case visualization of the proposal if adopted and a worst-case scenario of the proposal if rejected.

Prepare to Perform 6

Develop Presence

Speak with the kind of inflection, intonation, and other vocal dynamics we use in conversation. The richness of meaning in the spoken word begins with the voice.

Talk with the audience.

Speak like the audience is actually there–because they are! Listeners are people, not targets or "receivers." In a speech, you're not just transmitting information.

The term "communication" comes from the Latin *communis* or "common." Therefore, use your speaking voice to invite listeners into the message, to participate actively in the speech as a live communication event.

Practice conversational dynamics.

Speak with the same voice range you use in ordinary conversations. Your voice signals a lot about the content of the message and your attitude, all of which is vital information for a listener.

Speak for the ear.

Listeners will interpret the message based on how you sound. They are tuning in with their listening apparatus; your voice guides their interpretation more than any other single factor.

CULTIVATE A SPEAKING VOICE

Like radio announcers who develop an on-air voice, you need a speaking voice–a performance version of your ordinary voice. What's involved?

Resonance.

Tone quality. The audience gets a feel for the message through your speaking voice.

Range.

Pitch, volume, and rate. Dynamic changes register with listeners as energy, confidence, and enthusiasm.

Projection.

Vocal form and force. The audience needs to hear every word. Concentrate on intensity and articulation.

Public speaking is a performance. Your speaking voice is you in character, using your distinctive voice signature. Like an on-air voice, only use your speaking voice in public performance.

VARIETY

Variety in the treatment of the speech will be the great necessity. For in everything monotony is the mother of boredom.

–Cicero, *De inventione*, **Book I, Chapter XL.76**

A Speech is a "Talk"

To speak well, remember that a speech is a "talk."

Literally. A speech is not a "write," a "read," or a "recite."

You already speak well informally about things you know without writing them out. You know your stuff. Your voice is great. You don't memorize, you use your memory. That's what most listeners want to hear. They want you to talk with them. But lots of speakers write speeches and read them...poorly.

The fact that it's a "talk" doesn't mean you have to be nice. It's public speaking; you're not a therapist. The world has plenty of good, vehement conversations. So no matter what you have to say, you can say it better if you "talk" (not read or recite).

Is your voice bringing the message to life, or are printed letters putting the message to death?

Cultivate Your Speaking Voice

Transfer your familiar conversational vocal patterns into the public speaking context. A good speaking voice should be your voice, adapted to a public speaking context.

Bring your voice to life.

Practice performing your speech with vocal dynamics. You're speaking with the audience like you would in comfortable conversation. Nothing weird. Just you actually speaking, not droning.

- Oral Patterns. Pick good spots to start animating your voice. Practice the oral patterns, language, mnemonics, story forms, and dialogue you've prepared.

- Variety. Change speed, volume, and pitch. Match your voice to the message as you practice. Variation lets listeners hear your interest, which makes the message more interesting.

- Inflection. Punctuate the message with specific vocal emphasis. Voice inflection helps listeners distinguish your priorities. Pronunciation, dynamic changes, and dramatic pauses all contribute to good voice inflection.

Converse, don't rehearse.

Put the message in your own words as you speak. Change how you say things every time you practice. It helps to think through your message as you do with planned conversations. Just don't aim for exact wording and don't rehearse to memorize lines.

With good notes, you won't lose your place (see chapter 26, "Eye Contact and Notes"). They'll let you focus on performing one part of the speech at a time without distractions.

Speak to the back of the room.

Project your voice. Always assume someone at the back of the room is hearing impaired.

Face front, eyes up.

Direct your voice toward listeners. Don't speak to ceilings, floors, notes, or visuals. (It's fine to glance at a prompt–note, visual aid, etc.)

Be intense, not loud.

Focus your voice for distance. Concentrate on two major moves:

- Resonate. Bring sound from your throat forward until you can feel the resonance just behind your front teeth.
- Articulate. Open your mouth wider and be more deliberate about shaping the sound.

Breathe with control.

Increase capacity and control to project speech greater distances. You can project well at normal volume levels and even down to a stage whisper as long as you have enough air in your lungs and good breathing techniques.

Breathe from your belly (abdominal muscles) and your sides (intercostal muscles) to expand your breath control and capacity. At first this takes deliberate practice. Eventually, you'll be able to do it without paying attention.

Avoid the Drone

When you have something worth hearing, you can't afford to bore listeners. Most speakers in most ordinary situations today are droning away, even though many are smart people with important messages.

Will you join the majority of droners?

The drone of monotony.

> *Monotony comes in many forms.* Any unchanging vocal feature can cause monotony: steady tone, steady pace, steady volume, even a steady "sing-song" can bore listeners.

Fear constricts vocal dynamics.

> *Stage fright breeds monotony.* Why? The tightness compresses normal vocal variety.

Decompress your voice.

> *Speak more dramatically than feels comfortable and be deliberate about it.* Practice the strategies in this chapter to get a feel for your speaking voice under pressure.

You'll own a voice that engages people, even when you're nervous.

Tone of Voice

Listeners rely on your voice to get the meaning of the message. Words alone do not carry meaning. The single most important non-verbal factor is your tone of voice.

The Mehrabian 7-38-55 Rule says that non-verbal communication plays a much greater role in meaning than words: 7% of meaning depends on words (verbal), 38% on tone of voice, and 55% on all other non-verbal factors combined. Critics argue that Mehrabian's rule is a myth, based on a study of non-verbal communication and "liking..." that only applies in the context of the study. Of course they're technically right. The numbers only strictly apply to the scope of the study. But the rule is reliable in *principle* as it matches our experiences and complements other theories. For instance, we can say the words "I hate you!" and unmistakably mean "I love you!"

INTONATION AND EVALUATION

One of the means of expressing the speaker's emotionally evaluative attitude toward the subject of his [or her] speech is expressive intonation, which resounds clearly in oral speech (85).

~**Mikhail M. Bakhtin,** *Speech Genres and Other Late Essays*

Aristotle's Grudge

Work on your speaking voice. Why? Because of Aristotle's grudge.

Aristotle had a grudge against delivery. He didn't want delivery to matter so much. He called it "essentially, a matter of the right management of the voice to express various emotions...that suit various subjects."[1]

[1]**Aristotle,** *Rhetoric.*

He bemoaned that winning orators were the ones that kept the principles of delivery in mind and practiced them well. He also lamented:

> ...Delivery is—very properly—not regarded as an elevated subject of inquiry. Still, the whole business of rhetoric being concerned with appearances, we must pay attention to the subject of delivery, unworthy though it is, because we cannot do without it.

Aristotle would rather base the whole of every case on the facts and the proof of the facts. But he concedes delivery because it has a considerable effect on how audiences hear a speech.

Conclusion? If you've got good ideas and an ordinary speaking voice, no one will hear you.

Beating Common Voice Problems

Verbal pauses.

"I say 'uh' and 'um' too much." (Also: "like", "I mean", "you know", etc.)

Thinking well on your feet is a crucial speaking skill. When you're learning how to do it, you need more time to articulate thoughts in process. Verbal pauses buy time to think but we often use them without hearing what we're doing.

- Use a silent pause. To beat verbal pauses, practice speaking with a friend who can make some annoying noise every time you use your verbal pause(s), such as shaking keys. Once you can hear yourself using the pause, you'll soon be able to replace the verbal pause with a silent pause.

Too soft.

"I can't speak loud enough for people to hear me."

Do you have a quiet speaking voice? Don't try to be a loudmouth. But do work on projecting your voice.

- Focus on Intensity. A common technique is to speak into your hand. Begin with your hand directly in front of your mouth. Feel the resonance of your voice against your hand. Then move your hand further and further away, working to maintain the same intensity at a distance. Get accustomed to how your speaking voice sounds at higher intensity.

Too fast.

"I do okay when I practice, but when I get in front of people I talk really fast."

No constant speed, fast or slow, works well. Listeners need variety. Don't slow down in general; change your pace. Once you can slow down and speed up, you'll be able to use your voice for emphasis, like you already do in conversation.

- Plan pauses and change speeds. Think about how changes of pace and pauses can emphasize important parts of the message. Set up "speed limits" and "stop signs" in your speech plan, then practice pauses and changes accordingly.

Brain cramp.

"I get to a certain point in the speech and completely forget what I was going to say."

Memorization is the prime culprit that causes speakers to blank out. Try to remember specific words, details, or full sentences and you'll probably blank out at some point. But you can plan not to blank out and never worry about it again.

- Practice structure and main ideas. Audiences don't remember details, and, when you're speaking, neither should you. Practice to remember major moves in the structure of the speech. Use minimal notes and visual aids as prompts to make sure you remember where you're going (not the words you will say) and top priority material (not every detail).

Tongue-tied.

"I get my words mixed up or leave words out."

Words that work well written are often hard to say, especially under pressure. Listen for speaking rhythms. Think and hear how the message sounds when you say it, not how it looks or reads silently.

- Prepare speakable key phrases. Test language prep work you've done during speech design. Say things out loud. Revise main ideas and phrases until you can say them comfortably.

  If something doesn't feel right, change it on the spot! Don't try to be too clever. Keep your key phrases short, easy to say, and sweet to the ears.

Practice Out Loud

Is it okay to think through your speech? Sure. But you can't develop a good speaking voice by meditation.

In the hit musical *The Music Man*, Professor Harold Hill tries to defraud River City parents with the "Think System." All parents have to do is purchase an expensive instrument and an untrained child could supposedly learn to play just by thinking about it.

The "Think System" doesn't work for developing a good speaking voice either. *You have to practice out loud.*

Practice the speech out loud a number of ways. Don't be afraid to start, stop, and rework things in the process. (You're not rehearsing lines, but talking through the major moves of the speech.) Talk through parts of the speech with a friend casually. Tell them you've got a speech coming up and then practice a part of the speech you're still working out.

The important thing is to practice out loud, don't just think it through.

Include Some Impressions

A good way to build animation in your voice is to include vocal impressions when you relate a dialogue, example, or story in a speech—any time when someone else's voice comes into play.

Impression principles.

Begin with voices you can hear in memory. Once you get the hang of it you can create other voices.

- Play it straight for starters. Impressions can be fun and funny, but making fun is not the point. The goal is strong vocal dynamics.
- Approximate. The impression needs to be distinct from your voice, but not an identical copy of another person's voice.

Basic impressions.

Impressions help you to change your own voice and hear your voice better as you speak. In the process, you can animate, modulate, and articulate better in your own voice.

- "So they said to me..." Use a voice impression when someone is talking to you in your speech.
- "If she said it once, she said it a million times..." This type of voice impression captures a well-worn phrase just like the source has said it over and over again. Parents, bosses, coaches, and friends are good sources of such statements.
- "He said/she said..." Voice impressions work well when you can relate a dialogue between yourself and another person, or between two or more other people.

Speaking Voice Pitfalls

Flippant.

Conversational does not mean careless or dismissive in tone. The voice should indicate that the speaker takes the speech and audience seriously, even if the speech is delivered in a casual context or informal occasion.

Contrived.

An affected or overly dramatic voice is a distraction. In the process of cultivating a good speaking voice, the goal is to recover and develop the person's conversational dynamic range for public speaking performance.

Manuscript devotee.

Some cannot break away from manuscript speaking techniques. With rare exceptions, such speakers are doomed to believe they are communicating more than they are and to believing that any flaw in communication lies in the listening audience.

CONNECT IN PERSON

Learn to maintain direct eye contact with the audience through the entire speech. Direct, consistent eye contact is a defining feature of excellent delivery for public speakers. Eye contact is essential to public speaking as a planned conversation.

Direct eye contact.

Speak face-to-face with the audience. When you can look listeners square in the eye, you're on the road to good delivery as you'll be able to gauge how well the audience is engaging the message.

Consistent eye contact.

Make direct eye contact through the entire speech. Listeners should report that you talked with them face-to-face the whole time, even if you actually glanced at notes or visuals occasionally.

Communicative eye contact.

> *Use eye contact to maximize your transaction with listeners during the speech.* Humans send and receive messages simultaneously throughout a speech. With good eye contact, you can adjust to the audience as you speak and take advantage of all available communication channels.

EYE CONTACT

Delivery is wholly the concern of the feelings, and these are mirrored by the face and expressed by the eyes; for this is the only part of the body capable of producing as many indications and variations as there are emotions, and there is nobody who can produce the same effect with the eyes shut.

...Consequently there is need of constant management of the eyes, because the expression of the countenance ought not to be too much altered...but it is the eyes that should be used to indicate the emotions, by now assuming an earnest look, now relaxing it, now a stare, and now a merry glance, in correspondence with the actual nature of the speech. For by action the body talks, so it is all the more necessary to make it agree with the thought; and nature has given us eyes, as she has given the horse and lion their mane and tail and ears, to indicate the feelings of the mind, so that in the matter we are now considering the face is next in importance to the voice; and the eyes are the dominant feature in the face.

-Cicero, *De oratore*, **Book III, Chapter LIX.221-223**

Eye Contact: The Fear Factor

Why do we need to learn eye contact as a speaking skill?

Because most of us are not exhibitionists. Sure, we handle one-to-one eye contact pretty comfortably. But when we have many sets of eyes fastened on us, we tend to freak out, wondering "Why is everyone staring at me!?!"

Too much direct eye contact is a threat. Until we become experienced with it, eye contact from more than one or two people causes immediate anxiety.

The good news is that you can overcome the anxiety with practice, experience, and good planning.

Plan for Eye Contact

Premeditate delivery.

Think through, talk through, and walk through your speech with a face-to-face mindset. To generate consistent, direct eye contact demands deliberate attention and anticipation, just like many other performance activities.

Focus on facial expression.

Prepare to "hear" the messages on audience members' faces. When you lose eye contact, you deprive yourself of the most vital source of feedback available to a speaker.

Facial expressions work with audience eyes to respond to you.

Together they're a lifeline to audience interaction. At the same time, listeners are interpreting your face—the source and context of your voice and gaze.

Minimize notes.

Notes remind you what you are doing next, not what you are saying. You already know what you're going to say, just not exactly how you're going to say it. You've designed your message with care. So notes become a map of familiar territory, not turn-by-turn directions guiding you through a strange place.

Meet People's Eyes

To communicate best with the audience through listening as well as speaking during your presentation, you have to become comfortable with personal, direct eye contact.

You simply have to adjust to meeting listeners' eyes.

Make eye contact with one listener, then move to another. You're not looking deeply into their eyes.

In fact, staring at any one listener for more than a second or two will make them uncomfortable.

There is no particular pattern, but try not to leave anyone out or favor a specific part of the audience.

Some listeners will be more engaged and it may be hard to avoid favoring them. But make the effort to keep in contact with as much of the audience as possible.

Listener Sympathy and Non-Verbal "Mirrors"

Do audiences "feel" your presence as a speaker? It seems so. Autism research may help explain why.[2]

"Mirror neurons" seem to be a contributing factor to difficulties autistic people have connecting with others. Their mirror neurons don't fire. What happens when mirror neurons in your brain do fire? When you talk with someone else, they cause a sympathetic neurological response.

Mirror neurons that fire give you the cognitive ability to "feel" what someone else is doing in real time. It's a mental form of sympathy. It's as simple as smiling or waving back immediately when someone greets you, or mimicking someone just to annoy them. In more complicated forms, you cringe when you see someone else get hurt, you move involuntarily when watching a sporting event, or you get terrified in a horror movie precisely when you're supposed to.

For speakers, these same mirror neurons may begin to explain why audiences tend to mirror your behavior as a speaker. If you're engaged, they will be too. If you give eye contact, you're likely to get it. And if you're distracted and disengaged by notes, manuscript, visuals, or memorization, listeners will turn their attention elsewhere. Audiences mirror your presence. If you want them to engage the message, speak accordingly.

[2] J. H. G. Williams, A. Whiten, T. Suddendorf and D. I. Perrett. "Imitation, mirror neurons and autism", *Neuroscience & Biobehavioral Reviews, Volume 25, Issue 4, June 2001, Pages 287-295*

Why Speak Extemporaneously?

From ancient times to today, speech teachers have been saying, "speak extemporaneously." In other words, speak "from time." The speech is planned conversation–never written. The whole plan of this handbook favors *ex tempore* (extemp) preparation and delivery. But why?

Best communication.

> *Good speeches involve real transactions–two-way, simultaneous messages and responses.* Extemp gives the most contact points both ways through voice, eye contact, and other non-verbal channels.

Audience involvement.

> *Extemp offers more ways for you to get and keep audience attention.* Audiences mirror you, so direct eye contact helps them respond to you during the speech.

Speaking comfort.

> *Once you learn extemp delivery, no other type is as comfortable.* With extemp delivery, you'll connect with listeners and know it. It's easier to relax and enjoy speaking.

Credibility.

> *Extemp allows you to show your confidence and establish credibility.* People recognize and respect the skill.

Design Minimal Notes

You cannot have your nose in your notes and deliver your speech well. Prepare notes that encourage a dynamic speaking voice and good eye contact. Extensive notes and detailed speaking outlines suppress both.

Prompts and cues.

> *The best use of notes is to keep you within your basic game plan.* Notes can rescue you in a pinch and with good notes you never have to worry about losing your place or blanking out. Therefore, prepare brief cues (key words, short questions and phrases, not sentences) that can help you make your basic moves through the speech.

Seen, not held.

Good speaking notes are legible from a distance. The print should be easy for you to read from 6-8 feet away, whether you set them on a podium, table, or desk. Prepare them with a few key words, large lettering, and minimal details. A quick glance is all you should need to cue your next move.

Practice tool.

Notes do their best work before you speak. Rely on them heavily as you begin practice. As you move toward performance, depend on them only as prompts. By the time you speak, notes should become a safety valve that frees you to deliver with skill and confidence.

Flowchart or Outline?

Detailed Outlines Kill Eye Contact.

Should you create notes in the form of a flowchart or an outline?
Either is fine as long as you keep them both simple. Notes should be designed so that if you read every word aloud, the speech would be over in thirty seconds to a minute.

Use a basic flowchart or a simple keyword outline:

- Keep words to a minimum (no full sentences).
- Make all words and diagrams readable from a distance (6-8 feet).
- Limit number of pages or note cards.

EXCEPTION: Full sentences may be used for direct quotations, which should be read aloud.

TYPES OF DELIVERY

There are four major types of delivery. All can be used well and could be appropriate under certain conditions. In most contexts, extemporaneous (extemp) preparation and delivery provide superior communication.

	Delivery Format	Voice	Eye Contact	Prompts
ROTE MEMORY* (uncommon)	recite	memory rhythms	minimal	none
	FEAR: Blanking out			
MANUSCRIPT* (public figures, celebrities, preachers, and executives)	read	dull patterns	partial	speech text
	FEAR: Boring audience or losing place			
IMPROMPTU (routine in workplace contexts)	converse	informal "talk"	direct	no formal
	FEAR: Mistakes under pressure or wandering			
EXTEMP (common in professional and community contexts)	converse	formal "talk"	direct	prepared notes
	FEAR: Time (over/under) or forgetting details			

*People with extensive training, like actors, can manage memorization and manuscript presentation, performing them well.

Powerpoint "Handout" Notes

The "handout" print feature in Microsoft PowerPoint provides a simple way to develop speaking notes in a flowchart format, whether you're using the program for visual support or not.

1. Put your notes into a simple PowerPoint presentation, putting one major prompt/cue on each slide.
2. Using the "File" menu, go to "Print Preview."
3. In "Print Preview," go to the Print: drop-down menu and select either "Handouts (6 slides per page)" or "Handouts (9 slides per page)."
4. Print the handouts page(s) as speaking notes.

POWERPOINT NOTES SAMPLE

Dynamics of OrgComm

ORGANIZATIONAL STRUCTURE

How does Comm flow?
(formal & informal networks)

Dynamics of OrgComm

WORK ETHIC

How does OrgComm build productivity
(getting work done)

Dynamics of OrgComm

OFFICE POLITICS

Where are the power points?
(opportunities & obstacles)

Dynamics of OrgComm

SYSTEMS THEORY

Where are the relationships?
(interdependence & constraints)

Dynamics of OrgComm

PERSONNEL

How are staff being developed?
(human resources)

Dynamics of OrgComm

COMM ETHICS

What is the virtue structure?
(constructive workplace ethics)

Eye Contact and Note Pitfalls

A number of factors can get in the way of good eye contact and delivery. All diminish the quality of communication.

Partial eye contact.

> *A bit of eye contact is not enough.* Anxious speakers are particularly poor judges of the amount and quality of their eye contact. Manuscripts eliminate all but token eye contact for most speakers.

Memorization prohibits meaningful eye contact as the speaker can look at the audience generally, but can't make direct eye contact for fear of distraction.

Note dependence.

Detailed notes disrupt eye contact. When a speaker holds notes, the speaker and listeners may both be distracted, whether the notes are read or not.

Visual dependence.

Eye contact and delivery suffer when people speak to visual aids and computer monitors. This has become more common in workplace, professional, and academic presentations and will be treated in greater depth in chapter 7.

Five Delivery Myths

"Look just over the top of people's heads; they'll think you're making eye contact."

Nonsense. Our brains are designed to recognize whether someone is gazing at us directly, or merely looking in our direction. Listeners can tell the difference instantaneously.

"I deliver well when I really know the material."

Of course, if you don't know the material, the message is likely to fail. But all sorts of brilliant people are mediocre speakers. They're experts but can't speak well to save their lives.

"I can memorize the speech like an actor memorizes lines."

Maybe, but you shouldn't. Most people haven't memorized lines. But even if you have, a speech isn't a script. You are not a character in a play. This is real life. Memorization cuts off communication.

"Writing out the speech helps me so much!"

Only if you don't plan to present it. Writing out the speech commits you to specific words, memorization or pseudo-memorization, and brain cramps. It's a formula for droning.

"All I have to do is follow the PowerPoint."

Nope. Following the PowerPoint usually means reading lists of mind-numbing bullet points or a projected manuscript. You should be embarrassed, but you're not because you can't see the bored and sleeping listeners. You're staring at the screen.

PRACTICE PRESENCE

Maximize the rich context of face-to-face communication with the audience. In a world of media technologies, public speaking is an unusually rich channel. Through speaking presence, you coordinate message and audience interaction in delivery.

Engage listeners in person.

Put your whole self into connecting with the audience. You need to be "all there" to involve listeners in the message.

Embody the meaning.

What your body is doing needs to match what your mouth is saying. Attune yourself to the message, the audience, and the occasion. Listeners are depending on your integrated message–verbal and non-verbal–in the speech.

Perform the speech.

Public speaking is a communication event. The featured act is the direct connection between persons, the speaker and audience, around the message. You're the lead performer, the one who initiates the event and ensures its quality. Treat it that way.

Speaking Presence Better Than Technique

Listeners sense strong speaking presence when you are fully engaged "behind" the message; or "into" the message. Why?

Speaking presence takes heart.

It's more than a combination of delivery techniques. "Smooth operators" are skilled technicians, but empty. Their delivery is not matched by substance.

Speaking presence covers a multitude of problems.

You can make delivery mistakes without disrupting the message. Presence highlights content and connections between speaker and audience.

SPOKEN WORD AND WHOLE HUMAN BEING

Alone among all other sounds there is one that is particularly important for us: the spoken word. It ushers us into another dimension: relationship with other living beings, with persons. The Word is the particularly human sound which differentiates us from everything else... When I hear speech...the human being becomes qualitatively different from everything else. (14).

Ask the persona speaking with you to repeat the explanation he has just given, and it will be different. But you can reread a page. (44)

[The spoken word] is backed up by a person's whole being. (44)

~**Jacques Ellul,** *Humiliation of the Word*

How to Establish Speaking Presence

Put yourself in the best possible position to perform the speech. Learning to be a dynamic speaker demands a good delivery plan and practice.

Rely on conversational body language.

Your non-verbal speaking range should parallel conversational patterns. In conversation, most people use body language like gestures, posture, facial expression, and proximity to listeners in two distinct ways:

- Spontaneous. Conversational speech involves a full range of non-verbal communication that we just don't think about very much. We make faces, lean one way or the other, talk with our hands, or sit up or slouch without giving it a second thought. Good speaking means recovering much of our own range of spontaneous body language.

- Symbolic. Conversation includes intentional versions of all of the above. We use facial expressions to show our response; we gesture to show size, shape, direction, position, and motion; and we move in close or retreat on purpose.

All of this body language should contribute to your speaking presence as appropriate to the message, audience, and occasion—just as good conversationalists monitor their body language.

Block episodes.

Think of each speaking point as one scene in a play and plan your moves. Play directors block every scene to plan every movement, act, and line based on human motives.

In traditional drama, the players all face the audience. You should do the same kind of work to plan your speech; you're addressing the audience face-to-face.

Add reminders about critical moves to your speaking notes.

Practice your moves.

Do a physical walk-through of the speech with your notes. When you prepare for an extemporaneous speech, practice makes you familiar with your plan. You're not rehearsing lines; you're learning the speaking moves you'll make. From familiar ideas in a good structure, you can generate the message on your feet with a dynamic voice and good eye contact while you do it.

BODILY PRESENCE IN THE SPOKEN WORD

The oral word...never exists in a simply verbal context, as a written word does. Spoken words are always modifications of a total existential situation, which always engages the body. Bodily activity beyond mere vocalization is...natural and even inevitable. In oral verbalization, particularly public verbalization, absolute motionlessness is itself a powerful gesture. (67)

~**Walter J. Ong,** *Orality & Literacy*

Poise Means Composure (Not Perfection)

Speaking presence doesn't mean mistake-free speaking. It's about how you handle mistakes. It means you have poise. What's poise? Steadiness. Balance. Excellence under pressure. You're shockproof. You take a creative risk without announcing it. A mistake happens, you fix it, you move on. Without a word, you express that you always expect wrinkles and know how to manage them.

You're in control.

This registers with listeners as speaking presence, what they'll probably describe in a single word—confidence, energy, enthusiasm, or smart. They respond to your presence—as an immediate human connection about something that matters in their lives. Audiences expect composure, not perfection.

Speech Practice for Oral Memory

Try this form as a starting point to learn good habits and then adjust with experience. Veteran speakers need less structure to prepare well.

Talk through alone (but aloud).

> *Get a feel for how the speech feels sounded out.* Concentrate on what needs to happen in each segment—intro, episodes with transitions, and conclusion. "I'm going to begin this way..., then I'm going to say this..., etc." No need to do the speech as a whole. Stop and start to revise at will. As necessary, make adjustments in content, structure, support, etc.

Talk with someone else.

> *Discuss in conversation.* Work through the most important parts of the message and the most difficult ones. Practice eye contact and vocal dynamics in a conversational setting. Work through parts, not the whole. Interact with your listener(s) to get feedback and try adjustments. Continue revisions.

Walk through (with any props or visuals).

Work slowly through all the moves in the message. After you've blocked your moves in your mind, practice speaking through the message. Practice all the parts in order, stop and start. Work on connections, transitions, balance within the speech structure, visual timing, etc. Limit note dependence. Revise and adjust.

Run through.

Perform the whole message uninterrupted. Check for time and flow.

Follow your intuition on adjustments. If something doesn't feel right, change it (even if your time for practice is scarce). If possible, get at least one or two live listeners (people, not pets).

Review.

Pressure Points: Introduction, Transitions, Conclusion. As the performance approaches, master your moves for getting in, through, and out of the speech. Talk about and talk through these moves.

ORATORS BETTER THAN ACTORS

The whole of this department [delivery] has been abandoned by the orators, who are the players that act real life, and has been taken over by the actors, who only mimic reality. And there can be no doubt that reality beats imitation in everything.

~Cicero, *De oratore*, Book III, Chapter LVII.215

Remember with Your Body

Musicians, athletes, actors, and others rely on repetitions to prepare for performance when they can't control conditions or circumstances. When they practice, they do all the things they'll perform later *with their bodies*. They use practice repetitions to make adjustments and to incline their bodies to remember.

Performance physiologists and psychologists call these phenomena "muscle memory" and "mental mapping."

Under performance conditions, (e.g. when they're stressed, fatigued, and when unexpected things happen), the practice pays off. They don't have an exact script, but they have something better. A well-conditioned memory lets them excel by making good adjustments. As minds and bodies work in harmony, great performances result.

That's what speech practice for extemporaneous delivery is all about. When you practice with your mind, voice, and body, you establish presence. Use repetition to train yourself to remember the moves of the speech, not the words of a script. Then you'll perform better under stress.

Control the Speaking Space

When you perform, the speaking space is yours.

You want to own the venue so that you can produce the best, most dynamic connection for listeners. Speaking presence includes developing the ability to use the entire space (room, stage, etc.) for the purposes of the speech.

Don't get tied down to a podium, a table, or visual equipment. Eliminate obstacles that might hinder your ability to reach the audience. You want to be able to move through the whole speaking area comfortably.

Because of sound equipment and room arrangements, full access is not always possible and some speaking arrangements are very restrictive (like speaking from a podium at a head table). A speaker with good presence can perform well with significant limitations. But as much as possible, work as a free agent before the audience. Good speaking presence means you don't want or need to hide.

A Note on Podiums, Pulpits, and Tables

Podiums and pulpits are established sites of tradition...and make poor speakers feel safer.

Ignore them. Instead, engage listeners in-person to the greatest degree possible. Work free from everything that might come between direct access to listeners.

Of course, some formal occasions demand that you speak from a podium or lectern. Even in such cases, don't get attached to the apparatus. A speaker fixed to a podium can become a lonely person in a crowded room of sleepers. Honor the situation and remain active and vital for listeners.

Speaking Presence Pitfalls

Talking heads.

Don't be a statue. If you have a difficult time moving at first, plan a few deliberate moves. Try different tactics to expand your comfort zone. For instance, some people don't know what to do with their hands, but a pen or pencil gives them something to hold onto and their gestures improve.

Pacing, pinching, and primping.

Nervous patterns distract listeners. Practice to break the patterns. Stand and deliver from one place, then move to another (to shift audience perspective) and deliver there. Keep your hands away from your head; instead, use them for symbolic gestures or to manage visual aids.

No practice.

Thinking through your speech once in silence is not practice. Public speaking is a performance activity. You have to do more than read through your notes. Professionals do not always have time or means to do a full dress rehearsal of their speech, but people with good speaking presence find ways to fit in practice that aids performance despite busy schedules and imperfect contexts.

PERFORMANCE EXERCISES

Basic format.

In this set of exercises, speakers concentrate on delivery skills.

The speaker needs to focus attention on direct eye contact and voice in particular.

Purpose.

To expand the repertoire and ability to execute a wider performance range with greater flexibility.

Activities.

The three performance exercises suggested below can be used as starting points from which to work on specific delivery issues.

1. Table Topics with Delivery Emphasis.

   Toastmasters International is a voluntary association that helps members improve public speaking skills. One of their traditions is called "Table Topics"—an impromptu speaking exercise.

   Impromptu speaking is difficult in real world contexts. It's an excellent tool for building a good speaking voice and direct eye contact, though.

   To run Table Topics, someone in the group—the "Table Topics Master"—volunteers to bring simple impromptu topics to the table: index cards with topics written on them, a grab bag of "secret objects," or cards from a fun table game can serve as topics.

   The Table Topics Master announces the time limit, from thirty seconds to two minutes, and the game begins. Speakers stand at the head of a table or the front of a room and must fill the allotted time. The priority is on developing a lively speaking voice and consistent, direct eye contact.

2. Eye Contact Exercise: Shooting Gallery.

    a. Get a group of people together to work with you and speak on either impromptu topics or brief, prepared messages.

    b. Spread out across a whole room.

    c. At the start, listeners raise both hands.

    d. As you speak and meet a person's eyes, they lower one hand.

    e. By the end of the message, try to get all hands down.

Apply Beyond Speeches 7

Interactive Extensions

The basic public speaking skills under discussion so far in the book all have extensive applications in other communication contexts, particularly ones that transition speakers from formal presentation to deliberation and dialogue with other people, whether in conferences, committee meetings, or classrooms. This chapter is dedicated to dealing with the basic, interactive adaptations necessary and some of the more common interactive presentation contexts.

QUESTION & ANSWER SESSIONS

Develop a responsive, content-centered approach to question and answer (Q&A) sessions. Specific preparation and practices can help speakers enhance a message for listeners through Q&A.

Open conversation.

Listeners become active, verbal participants. You share control of the agenda and can ask listeners clarifying questions in the process. The setting becomes less formal and everyone tends to become more animated and involved.

Add and interpret content.

Speakers can supplement and explain the message. A well-designed speech draws questions that will invite you to explain material that you didn't have time for during the speech. Questions give you insight into audience understanding of issues, which can help you respond better.

Increase audience attention.

People pay closer attention to Q&A responses than to speeches. When someone asks a question, people are more interested in the response than they would be if they heard the same thing in a speech. The audience stimulus and the relational component can add drama ("How will they respond to that?!).

Conduct a Q&A Session

A good Q&A session takes preparation and leadership. It's more than just stopping a speech and asking for questions.

Anticipate.

Predicting what to expect is the most important factor in Q&A quality. When you know your own message and the audience, guessing the likely content and conduct of the session becomes easier.

- Questions. Frame the questions you think will, should, and could be raised. You won't get all the questions you anticipate. You'll get a few you couldn't have guessed.

  By itself, the exercise strengthens your mental agility with the issues and will help your prepared remarks as well.

- Questioners. From whom do you expect questions? Certain people are bound to ask questions–what are they likely to ask? Others are likely to be silent. Of the remainder, who might ask what questions?

  You need to do this detailed work to prepare yourself for potential opportunities and problems. To conduct yourself professionally, remember that everyone will be measuring your responses even if they don't ask a single question.

- Response Options. Review alternative ways to respond to the questions and questioners. Make contingency plans and work through the best responses.

  Know your strong and weak points. Think through how to answer the best/toughest questions that should be asked in the most challenging ways (whether they come or not).

Listen and check.

Once a Q&A session begins, take nothing for granted. Don't trust your listening skills. Don't jump to conclusions. Take time to hear each question and make sure you understand. You don't need to confirm your understanding of every question, but if you have any doubt about the question, ask for clarification.

Respond to the whole audience.

Answer questions as if you were giving a mini-speech. Under good conditions, listeners appreciate being included. When a Q&A session gets rough, it's critical. You don't ever want to let one listener "lock-on" to you and dispense with the rest of the audience. Make it a practice to address answers to the whole group, never just one listener.

Delivery Skills in Q&A

Live Q&A is a dramatic, dynamic event. In face-to-face Q&A performance, extemporaneous delivery skills become even more important than in a formal speech. Q&A performance has a huge impact on your credibility.

Many speakers, especially politicians and celebrities, deliver prepared remarks easily but sound incompetent during Q&A. Impromptu exercises and extemporaneous delivery pay huge dividends in Q&A because you're so much better prepared to think well on your feet.

Voice.

Vocal agility allows you to pause during Q&A, both for thought and for emphasis. Developing oral patterns allows you to maintain command in responses and to exercise self-control.

Eye contact.

Some of the most important work you do in Q&A depends on direct eye contact. In fact, you facilitate a good Q&A session almost entirely with your eyes.

For instance, eye contact is critical to responding to the whole audience (rather than getting locked-on with one questioner) and inviting other listeners into the conversation (rather than allowing one person to dominate the questions).

Presence.

Your position with the audience and posture are vital to managing Q&A well. For instance, it's much more important to orient yourself toward the person asking a question. Move close to listen carefully, then reposition yourself to answer with a full audience view.

Strengthen Your Case in Q & A

Give listeners more than mere opinions when you respond. Provide support. When you do, your responses will continue to build a content-rich case for your message. Remember that support includes good reasons, evidence, illustrations, examples, and/or even a brief story.

No need to state every possible source of support in Q&A. Point to the support and add more detail if people ask a follow-up question.

A case building response.

- Sample Question: "You said that it's hard to find a place where people can be certain they're not under some sort of electronic surveillance. But can't we be pretty certain that we're not under surveillance in our own homes?"

- Response: "It's reasonable to assume that most people are not under electronic surveillance in their own homes. But that's not the point. We can't know that we're not under surveillance, because if we were, we probably wouldn't know it. For example, Tom Clancy published the novel *Patriot Games* with reference to common surveillance technology already available in 1987. The film-version came out in 1992 with a scene using a nearly-invisible fiber-optic camera that could be used anywhere on the planet that you can hide."

Support against an interrogator.

How do you respond to the audience member who would dominate the whole session like an interrogator? This person is sometimes curious and intrigued—"just so interested!" Other times, the person may strike a competitive pose or be hostile.

Many listeners will be supportive of attempts you make to constrain the dominator and involve others in the discussion. They'll even help if you let them.

When a questioner asks a third or fourth follow-up question, you can say a number of things to move on with the help of others:

- Before answering: "I see that others have questions. I'll respond to this and then take questions the rest of you may have."
- After answering: "What do some of the rest of you think? What questions do you have?"
- After answering: "Now I'd like to take a question from someone who hasn't had an opportunity yet."

In most cases, listeners will work with you and get involved themselves.

Response Guidelines

Lead Q&A by keeping the focus on the content and maintaining control of your own speaking agenda. Well-considered, well-executed responses set a good tone for constructive interaction.

Give direct answers.

Make it a habit to answer what's asked. Establish patterns of reliability and be true to your word. Direct answers are very valuable, and a reputation for dependability is essentially unrecoverable once it's lost.

Truthfulness doesn't demand that you tell all in exhaustive detail—especially in public contexts. But make indirect and incomplete answers exceptional. Avoid patterns of evasion, equivocation, and strategic ambiguity that lead to deceit.

Stay on topic.

Give a solid, focused answer, and then stop. A question is not an invitation to give another whole speech. There are fewer crucial details than you think during a Q&A session. Give your mouth a break and wait for another question.

Qualify type of answer.

What's the level of your answer? Let listeners know that your response is well-supported, a good alternative among many, or a personal preference. It's okay to speculate in an answer that takes you outside of your prepared content, but if you're speculating, say so.

Learn to Say "I Don't Know"

You don't know everything. Why pretend? A person might occasionally ask a question they know has no answer, just to test you.

One reliable indicator of knowledge is when a person is comfortable saying, "That's beyond what I know. You would have to ask [specific person or sort of person] to get an answer to that."

It's even honorable to say, "I should know, but I don't." In many workplace contexts, a common version of this response is, "I don't know, but I'll find an answer for you."

If you find yourself responding this way all the time, you spoke too soon. But to perform well in Q&A you have to learn to simply say, "I don't know."

Dealing with Hostile Questions

There's always a possibility that hostile questions will come.

They may be hostile to the message, hostile to the process or context, or hostile to you personally. It's hard to tell what might be causing the hostility. But whatever the source, here are a few response tips:

Never assign motives.

Avoid the, "You're just asking that because..." response. You may suspect motives or even know them directly, but always try to offer a public response based on the content of the question, not the cause.

Deflect personal attacks.

If someone uses an accusatory tone or makes a direct allegation against you personally, avoid a response. Instead, reinterpret the question as a content question and deal with it as carefully as possible or ask for other questions.

Note: Keep the session focused on the content and the audience as a whole. You may respond with active non-verbals, though. By avoiding personal reaction, you stand against the hostility and reject its legitimacy. Move on as quickly and decisively as possible, without being flippant or condescending.

Invite others into discussion.

When a hostile question comes, complete your response then prompt other perspectives that likely exist in the audience. Use a phrase like: "You've heard a concern about what we've been discussing. What viewpoints are some of the rest of you working from?" or "You've heard my response. What questions do others have?"

Equity between listeners is an important value. At least some other listeners are likely to support it against a hostile questioner.

Q&A Sanity Savers

When you've presented remarks and are fielding questions, usually you moderate the Q&A session. Indicate that you will try to answer questions from as many people as possible within the time constraints. If multiple people have questions, you set the order.

People don't always ask question well. They're thinking out loud and having a difficult time putting thoughts into words. Here are some tips for handling awkward or suspect questions:

Restate convoluted questions.

Allow the questioner to finish. Then take a minute to summarize the question as you understand it. Check with the person who asked the original question to confirm your interpretation before responding.

Reinterpret closed questions.

Some questions come in an either/or (a fixed/alternative) format. In many of these cases, a simple "yes" or "no" will not do.

The person asking may be struggling to frame the question. Or someone may be trying to force you into a no-win answer.

Either way, as the speaker you can (and should) reinterpret the question as an open question, and then respond.

- Question: "Are you for or against Internet censorship?"
- Answer: "The question of Internet censorship is difficult, because it begins with defining who owns the Internet and how it's regulated…" (then address the open question clearly).

Answer compound questions in your order.

When someone asks three questions in one statement, you don't have to answer in the order they were asked.

Simply explain how you will proceed: "I'll start with the last question first, then go to the first one. After that, I might need some help remembering the middle question."

Q&A Pitfalls

Listeners come to Q&A sessions with higher expectations. They want coherent answers. The major Q&A pitfalls discussed below fail the "coherent answer" test.

The non-answer.

Every question deserves a response, not necessarily an answer. If you can't answer, say so. Complicated drivel to avoid an answer is still drivel.

It's better to say, "That's a good question, but it's difficult to answer." Or–if true–to say, "I cannot answer that question, because..." (if the limitations can be spoken). When he was serving during the first Iraq War in the early 1990s, General Colin Powell did a masterful job of this at press conferences, often saying something like, "I'm not going to answer that question while our troops are involved in combat operations. The answer might put our soldiers' lives at greater risk."

Digression.

Respond to what has been asked. Digressions are no more welcome in Q&A than they are in a speech. If you must digress, do it in boring, harmless personal conversations.

Pontification.

Don't be a pompous windbag. Demonstrate your knowledge by the precision, brevity, and content of your answers, not by an air of self-assurance. No matter who you are, there aren't many people who think they're much below you. If you talk down, your answers will likely miss the audience.

LEADING DISCUSSIONS

Get group members involved in thinking and working together with significant ideas. Discussions can be stand alone events. They are also vital to decision-making, learning (teaching and training), and other meeting contexts.

Full participation.

Create a climate where everyone is invited and expected to contribute. Participation is a defining feature and a guiding practice for good discussions. Well-designed discussions cultivate widespread involvement.

Content focus.

Build discussion around issues and ideas. A planned discussion is about questions that are worth extended group conversation. Good processes advance good discussion patterns, but good procedure is not the goal. The goal is a shared pursuit of truth and knowledge, good ideas, and wise decisions.

Concrete outcome.

Guide interaction for a specific purpose. A good discussion should be geared toward producing a certain type of tangible result. The specific outcome cannot be predetermined; that's what the discussion should yield.

Types of outcome include: decisions, insights, plans, policies, practices, clarification of issues, nominations, elections, appointments, etc.

How to Prepare A Discussion

Craft group interaction toward the purpose of the meeting. Prepare carefully and develop specific skills to cultivate participation and guide discussion. Good leadership involves framing the process and collaborating with the group to generate content.

Invention.

Find the question(s). The quality of the discussion depends on the quality of the questions. Good discussion starts with good questions.

- Organizing Question: The main issue. The issue is the organizing question on which the discussion turns–the "must answer" question for the discussion to be fruitful.
- Contributing Questions: The division or breakdown. You often need to divide the organizing question into smaller questions that lead to it. This breakdown gives you a list of questions that contribute to the purpose of the discussion.
- The Starting Question: The opener. A question used to launch the discussion, usually one of the contributing questions. The starting question needs to engage all participants and spark their active involvement.

Arrangement.

Plan a progression of questions. Put questions in order to chart a course that can achieve the discussion's purpose. Basic question patterns are listed below. Tailor them to match the contours of your situation.

- Problem-Solving. What's the problem and how do we solve it? Discussion would revolve around questions to define the problem, consider possible solutions, and recommend a particular solution.
- Determine Cause. Why did this happen? Discussion might start with considering the effect and then turn to identifying reasons.

- Formulate Policy. What should we do next? Whether recommending or deciding, a policy discussion is about defining specific courses of action.

- Learn Ideas. What is this and what does it mean/do? Discussions of discovery and creation are collaborative attempts to understand, define, and generate new ideas.

Style.

Frame the questions and types of responses. Refine questions to invite significant contributions from a wide spectrum of participants.

- Open Questions. You have to use questions that invite multiple good responses.

- Desired Responses. Specify whether you want opinions, experiences, examples, lists, reasons, etc.

Memory.

Write out questions that connect with participants. It's your job to put questions in familiar terms, common contexts, and memorable forms. Good discussion begins in familiar territory, connected to people's experience, knowledge, and expectations–their active memory. You can take a discussion to new places, but the journey has to start at home.

Delivery.

Guide the discussion with listening. The quality of interaction depends on how well you listen as it shapes your responses. As a discussion leader, you need to use good delivery skills as discussed in chapters 5-8, plus active listening skills.

- Open The Floor. Welcome participation by how you listen. Engage participants actively as they speak. Make interruptions rare.

- Summarize Occasionally. Note how contributions relate, progress, contrast, etc. Reminders help a group as discussion progresses. Depending on your role, you may be more inclined to describe the discussion or interpret it. Either form of summary can be appropriate.

- Position Yourself Strategically. Move to listen well and encourage others to listen. In many cases, this means moving away from the speaker to the other side of the room or meeting area to help the speaker direct their voice toward a larger segment of the group.

Frame Questions for Discussion

The single greatest factor in the quality of discussion may well be the quality, in form and content, of the discussion questions.

But how can you guide a discussion when a good discussion means that other people are doing most of the talking? Well, you're asking the questions, aren't you?

Remember this basic principle: "Whoever asks the questions controls the conversation."[1]

[1]Kenneth Burke, literary critic and rhetorical theorist, is often credited with this statement.

There are thousands of practical applications of this truth, but leading a good discussion is one of the best. As you become more skilled at leading, you will be able to use discussions more and more to help people learn together, solve problems together, and make wise decisions together.

Employ Open and Closed Questions

The single most important skill you can learn in order to lead discussions is the ability to differentiate between an "open" and a "closed" question.

Closed questions.

> *Closed questions prompt single, fixed answers: yes/no, right/wrong, good/bad, either/or.* They generally involve "to be" verbs (is, are, was, were, be, being, been), and variations on "do" and "can." Closed questions stop discussion.
>
> If you ask closed questions, you may think that participants are disinterested or unresponsive. You'd be wrong. The lack of response to such questions is predictable. Hardly anyone wants to respond to closed questions, even if they know the answer.

Closed questions are useful for transitions or closing discussion. For example, you say, "Does anyone have any other questions or comments?" In most cases, people will answer "no" in their own minds, say nothing, and allow you to move the session along.

Open questions.

Open questions invite people into discussion and allow a wide variety of good answers. They generally begin with "what": "what are some ways that...," "what do you think about...," or "what are some reasons why..." An open question is phrased to ask for opinions, ideas, examples, and responses that enable many people to contribute.

Open questions say, "Please let us know what you think." Pose them in a way that invites participation and welcomes input. A well-framed open question tells people that they can think out loud without fear of error or reprisal. They can try to make a serious contribution.

Sample closed and open questions.

On Electronic Surveillance...

- Closed. "Can you be certain that you're not under electronic surveillance? Are you under surveillance right now?"
- Open. "What are some places where you could you be certain that you're not under electronic surveillance? What about now?"

On Intelligent Life Beyond Earth...

- Closed. "Is there intelligent life beyond Earth?"
- Open. "What might intelligent forms of life be like beyond Earth?"

Sample discussion prompts.

These are different kinds of open questions to generate discussion.

- Examples. What kinds of interviews might be used in different jobs and professions to screen candidates?
- Opinions. Which interview factors play more important roles in hiring decisions? How should people prepare?

- Experiences. What are some difficult interview situations you or your friends have been through? What advice would you give based on your experiences?

- Reasons. What are some reasons why so many people go into interviews unprepared?

- Lists. You are a retail customer for a number of product and service companies today. If you had to work in that line of business, pick three you would seriously consider and three whose job offers you would decline.

Discussion Killing Questions: "Guess My Answer"

"Guess my answer" questions are a species of closed questions. They are confirmed discussion killers.

A "guess my answer" question has a specific answer already in the discussion leader's mind (it may have many parts). Nothing is really up for discussion.

Participants sense this and shut up, even if they might know the answer.

Build Active Participation

Initiate discussion with proactive practices. Unlike personal discussions, group discussions rarely emerge spontaneously. The main challenge is to generate broad participation. In most discussions a few people do all the talking. But less talkative people have good contributions to make and input that is often needed in important discussions.

Expect participation.

> *Coordinate everything you do and say to encourage full involvement.* From the start of the discussion, state your expectation and invite people to contribute.

Use discussion catalysts.

> *Put questions in formats that make participation easy and safe.* Use creative discussion patterns that do not focus exclusively on "Q&A style" discussion in which all input is directed toward the leader.

Direct traffic.

Set clear ground rules to guide participation. Good discussion gives everyone a chance to contribute. It doesn't give everyone a chance to say whatever they want, whenever they want.

For instance, you can set patterns for input (i.e. "let's go around the room") and invite people to comment in the order that you recognize their desire to speak (whether by raising hands or informal gestures).

As the rule enforcer, it's also your job to set boundaries for extroverts and encourage input from introverts. You have at least two major roles:

- Protect Participants. When someone contributes, you have to protect them from interruption or personal attack. You need to jump in immediately and say something like:

  "Excuse me, we need to hear the rest of what our colleague has to say. Then we'll be able to hear from others..."

  or

  "Strike the last! We'll have time to discuss the issues in a minute, but we're going to stick to the issues, we're not getting personal!"

- Prevent Domination. In every discussion, some people will dominate unless you work hard to involve the whole group. Forget motives and personalities; deal with the situation functionally. A basic form can be used in a variety of ways. And note, if you have a non-stop talker, it's legitimate when they take even a quick breath to break in and say:

  "Thanks, Domino." Then turn and address other participants, "What have some of the rest of you been thinking about regarding this issue?"

  When moving the discussion to a new topic, you can also use a phrase like: "I'd like to hear from some of you that haven't had much input yet..."

Make no apology for reaching out to the full range of participants. Be thoughtful, gracious, an unequivocal about including others.

"Engage in Five"

To cultivate participation, get group members involved actively from the start. We make quick judgments about whether we're supposed to interact or just sit and listen passively.

Participation principle.

Get every participant involved in meaningful interaction within the first five minutes of a session.

Do you want to cultivate an interactive climate? Don't lecture early. If you want interaction, don't provide ten minutes of background. Don't review. Don't say you want people to participate and then lecture for the first ten minutes of a session.

Participation practice.

Open with a meaningful, interactive task that everyone can do with at least one peer. Every person should be able to contribute through speaking briefly and listening actively.

Start with broad interaction as a signal so that you won't need to ask for participation, you can just keep practicing it. On the other hand, if you say that you'll be glad to be interrupted and answer questions, expect the silence of the grave (which is, apparently, what you want).

Ask Follow-Up Questions

Encourage participation with good follow-up questions.

A follow-up question, especially one that invites a participant to amplify a brief comment, advances the discussion in a number of ways simultaneously.

First, it demonstrates that you're really listening. You understood the comment and your follow-up invites the speaker to continue a train of thought they started.

Second, it affirms involvement. In many cases the follow-up question is directed at a less-talkative group member who has given only a brief comment. The follow-up takes the comment seriously.

Third, it highlights content. Instead of congratulating the speaker for speaking, it focuses attention on the message. The follow-up privileges substance.

Discussion Catalysts

You'll need more than good questions to get broad participation. The following ideas will help you engage the whole group through thought processes that invite everyone to participate.

Write before speaking.

Ask people to write a personal response to an open question. Allow time for people to think and write. After a few minutes, invite responses. Options include:

- Poll everyone. (Especially for small groups or short answers).
- Select randomly. (E.g., everyone born in a certain month).
- Pick a few less-talkative people. (Before opening the discussion.)

Pre-written responses guarantee that people have something to say, which is less intimidating for most. You get a variety of perspectives, not just quick responders. Even if everyone doesn't talk, all become active participants.

Partners.

Pose a question to be discussed with an immediate neighbor in the group. One-on-one conversations prompt a wide variety of responses, including ones that wouldn't have come from either partner individually. You can move to a full group discussion and ask for input from partners, or move the discussion into small groups.

Small groups.

Create groups and give them a discussion question or problem. Small groups are also particularly good for quick brainstorming sessions. Select spokespersons and have a number of groups report back to initiate a full group discussion on the question or problem (all groups in a small discussion setting).

These discussion catalysts can be usefully combined. For instance, you can move a discussion group through all three stages before discussion. The following provides a basic example of how a progression of discussion questions can be arranged to lead a group.

- Intro: Catalyst (Starting Question). What groups of people do you think are getting the most sleep these days? Why?
- Problem: Division (Contributing Question). Physicians, especially sleep specialists, have been saying people aren't getting enough sleep. What are some reasons why we should worry if we're sleep deprived?
- Cause: Division (Contributing Questions). What kinds of things put pressure on people to reduce how long they sleep? What other sorts of long-term factors disrupt good sleep patterns?
- Solution: Issue (Controlling Question). What are some realistic, practical ways that people like us could significantly improve our sleep patterns for long-term health?

Discussion Leading Pitfalls

Don't put a person on the spot.

Allow time for thought. If you just throw a question out, avoid calling on an individual. Let people volunteer.

If you allow ample time to think and perhaps give people a chance to write down an idea or discuss the question with a partner, then you can call on them personally.

Don't answer your own questions.

Wait patiently–for at least fifteen seconds! Inexperienced leaders often close off what might have been a great discussion by answering their own questions rather than waiting just a few more seconds for responses.

Don't humiliate participants.

Affirm participation and invite other responses. If you challenge comments on the spot, don't expect anyone else to say much.

Who wants to risk public rejection? Instead, offer a simple "thank you," without comment on the content. Then look to another participant for input. When other participants offer more helpful comments, comment on their input *without* demeaning earlier remarks.

MEETING MANAGEMENT

Design and lead meetings that get work done and make the most of participants' knowledge and skills. Meetings are crucial to civic, community, and organizational life, but they often fail to deliver on their potential and instead generate frustration.

Establish the purpose.

Make the group's task clear. People need to know the group's objective and their role in the meeting.

Set the agenda.

Organize the meeting to serve its purpose(s). You're the agenda-setter. Keep all items off the agenda that can be done in any other good way to make the most of the group's potential. You should be confident about why each item is necessary for the group and what you expect to accomplish at each stage of the meeting.

Run the agenda.

> *Keep the group on task.* Initiate and guide the group's work with care. Digressions, distractions, and loss of focus are all your fault.

Your role is to put others in a good position to contribute. If the chair does all the work, good people will check out.

Why Meet?

In the non-profit world full of meetings, the saying goes, "Meetings are up, productivity's down!" If that's true, then why meet at all?

Decision quality.

> *Groups always make better decisions.* Except when decisions rely solely on sophisticated technical expertise, the quality of group decisions consistently surpasses that of any individual in the group. For example, even highly-skilled medical specialists work in teams to decide on the best treatments for difficult cases.

Group buy-in.

> *Good meetings build member commitment.* When groups practice collaborative decision-making, group members report higher levels of commitment and support for the decisions than for decisions handed down by executive fiat.

- Buy-In Fraud. The benefits of even moderately effective group meetings are so strong that leaders are tempted to gain the benefits fraudulently.

- The Scenario: A leader has made a predetermined decision, but doesn't announce it publicly to the group. The leader calls a "decision-making meeting" at which group members are led to believe that a decision has yet to be made.

The leader, either directly or through an associate, attempts to manipulate the meeting to arrive at the predetermined decision. In many cases, the leader thinks the strategy has worked, and then wonders why the participants do not seem to be responding with the expected commitment and productivity.

Duh!

Productivity.

> *Decisions made by groups build positive energy.* Group meetings and decisions generate greater productivity from members when compared with productivity levels without meetings. For instance, the social pressure of needing to complete a task for next week's meeting is a powerful motivator.

But Why Am I at this Meeting?

"I don't know why they sent me to this meeting!" Millions of people have been thinking this in meeting rooms all over the planet today.

As chair, it's your job to answer this question early and often, framing the purpose by what you say and by what you do in the meeting. People's time is precious. Make every minute count with content that matters.

Don't meet about anything that could be done as well or better in another communication format.

Design meetings to make the best use of groups, particularly deliberating and decision-making. Members do not need to be active every moment. Listening is a legitimate activity and a mark of wisdom. Just make sure that most of the listening people do in your meetings is tied to the purpose of the meeting.

Meeting Purposes

Identify the purpose of the meeting. Make clear to the group what type of meeting this is and what role they are playing. For instance, if a group is tasked to make recommendations but members think they have decision power, frustration and cynicism may result.

Consider the following three basic types of meeting (some meetings are more complex, incorporating all three types in a single agenda).

Information.

> *A person or group presents material to the group.* In some cases, a Q&A session is part of the meeting, but the group is simply receiving a message. Dynamics and chair responsibilities are limited.

Consultation.

Deliberate and make a recommendation to a decision maker (person or group). The group meets as an advisory committee and may produce anything from a simple recommendation to an extensive report. The meeting involves no binding, decision-making component.

Decision-making.

Deliberate and make binding decisions with accountability for its decisions. The group enacts decisions or delegates action items to others (people or other groups).

Consultation meetings and decision-making meetings are collaborative and participatory. You have to manage group dynamics in both to stimulate and guide interaction.

Prepare a Meeting

Framing a good meeting means using basic design elements to execute a good meeting plan. The prime planning tool is the agenda. Leading demands good public speaking and discussion skills combined with specific skills to moderate.

Invention.

Identify content issues and agenda items. List the topics you need to cover in the meeting. Note why each item belongs on the agenda, who has responsibility for the item, and the process by which each issue is to be resolved in the meeting.

Arrangement.

Build a working agenda. The working agenda is your detailed plan for the meeting.

- Climate Issues. Consider the context in which the meeting will take place. Meeting conditions play a significant role in its progress and results.

  a. *Roster.* List the members you expect to attend. Also note guests and support people who will participate.

b. *Time and Place.* Set the time frame and location. Make sure that both are adequate to accommodate the work to be done in the meeting.

c. *Supporting Materials.* What information will members need in advance? What handouts and other materials will be provided at the time of the meeting? (e.g. agenda, reports, background information, etc.)

- Order. Organize the meeting structure to get the work done. Take three main factors into account:

a. *Symbolic.* Certain agenda items have significant symbolic value. Many meetings begin or end with culturally important activities that remind members of the core mission and reinforce group values.

b. *Tactical.* Coordination of agenda items sometimes determines order. Some items cannot be considered until other items are considered and resolved. Perhaps a particular item may involve a guest, who can only join the group at a certain time during the meeting.

c. *Strategic.* Top priority items should be given prominence, both in order and in time allotted.

Style.

Frame agenda items. Develop specific plans for each one.

- Purpose. State the action to be taken. What should the group accomplish during this agenda item? Will the group discuss and deliberate a new idea? Does a decision need to be made or a recommendation penned?

- Item Leaders. Assign leadership of the group for the agenda item. In many cases the chair leads, but in some cases you may delegate a particular agenda item to another group member (e.g. a vicechair or committee chair).

- Decision Process. Consider the best decision making process for the particular group and agenda item. Common options include:

a. *Chair Decision.* In many contexts, accountability for decisions rests with the chair. The group serves a consultative role and makes recommendations. You make the decision.

b. *Majority Vote.* The chair may call for a voice vote, raised hands, a roll-call vote, or a secret ballot.

c. *Consensus.* The chair leads an interactive meeting process to identify a group consensus point.

d. *Deferral.* The chair suspends discussion. Therefore delaying a decision until a future meeting. In formal meetings, the group can decide to "table" a motion that is under discussion to accomplish a similar purpose. Deferral can be wise when uncertainty or divisions are severe and a decision is not necessary.

- Time. Allocate a specific amount of time for the item. Time limits help chairs move agendas effectively. Without time limits, some groups never get through even the essential work of a given meeting.

Memory.

Decide how to record decisions made and future action items. The value of many meetings is lost because people can't remember what was decided or who is supposed to do what before the next meeting.

If the group doesn't already have an established pattern for notes or minutes, decide what kind of record you'll use (see "Meeting Record Options"). Ordinarily, you should assign someone else to take notes and produce the record so that you can give full attention and energy to leading the meeting.

People use a variety of methods to document meetings. Note that the meeting record has an impact on how people interact in a meeting.

- No Record. In fact, not every meeting has or needs a record. The outcome of informal meetings is often real, but undocumented.

- Chair Memo. Many smaller meetings (e.g. staff meetings, sub-committees, etc.) can be recorded by a simple memo from the chair immediately after the meeting.

- Court Reporter. Occasionally a meeting, or a portion of a meeting, requires word-for-word documentation. Beyond the courtroom, this method is often used in disciplinary contexts and when questions of legal liability are prominent.

- Roberts' Rules Minutes. Perhaps the most common, traditional form of minutes, Roberts' Rules of Order minutes records deliberation and decisions. Names are attached to formal motions, including who moved and seconded the motion, as well as to various points made in discussion.[2]

[2]Henry Martyn Robert, *Robert's Rules of Order.*

- Group Memory. When a group is generating ideas through brainstorming or other group processes, an informal record can be produced, usually based on ideas recorded on boards, charts, etc.

- Decisions/Action Items. A simpler form of minutes notes only formal decisions of the group without identifying names. This form usually includes a summary of discussion and a rationale for decisions. Action items attach names to work projects assigned by the group.

Delivery.

Chair the meeting. Use the working agenda for speaking notes and lead the group through the meeting, relying on your basic public speaking skills, Q&A skills, and discussion leadership skills.

- State Expectations. Introduce the meeting with specific guidelines to facilitate and coordinate the group's work. Do this briefly, but explicitly—don't take it for granted. You'll help people focus on roles and responsibilities in the meeting.

- Set Limits. As you approach each item, explain how the meeting will proceed. Include time limits, the significance of the agenda item, and the group's role (receiving info? deliberation? recommending? making a decision?).

- Move The Agenda. No one else can make the meeting work. You have to coordinate discussion and decision making, by launching interaction and decisions processes.

Moving and Shaking a Meeting

What is a "mover and shaker" anyway?

If you're going to be a good chair leading and managing meetings well, you have to move and shake. In a meeting that matters (and don't meet if it doesn't matter), you'll need all your public speaking skills and more to make the meeting work.

Moving.

To chair well, you need to be assertive. You can be quietly assertive or take a more "rah-rah" attitude. Either way, you set the pace for the meeting. You move it.

Mastery of the basic art of public speaking will provide the mindset and basic abilities. To move the agenda, you have to set the pace and tone with your voice, your eye contact, and your presence.

Shaking.

Once you get the meeting moving, you'll occasionally need to "shake" the group. It's your job, and yours alone, to keep members on task and call them out to make a decision or to work better together.

Shaking will take all your discussion leading skills and more. As coach, law enforcement, and referee, you'll be thinking on your feet, raising questions, and delivering the word (or exercising restraint) simultaneously.

Preventions & Interventions

Two simple, effective practices can help you lead meetings more effectively:

Preventions.

Ground rules stated in advance. Talk through expectations for behavior in the meeting and explain how the group does its work. For example,

"Let's work 'off the grid' today. Please silence your phones and put them away. Our meeting will last 45 minutes and we'll all have time then to check messages after the meeting. Thank you."

Standard preventions include walking through the agenda, ground rules about participation, reminders about breaks, meeting record, decision processes, etc.

Interventions.

Chair-guided course corrections. Interrupt and interject at key points during the meeting to address problems with difficult people or groups (e.g. bullying, dominating, side conversations, etc.). You may also need to prod the group to complete its work. If necessary, revise the agenda to accommodate meeting dynamics, adjust to changing conditions, and take advantage of emerging opportunities.

Unanimity, Consensus, and Common Consent

Explaining the process and goal of decision-making meetings is crucial to good group work. Our expectations for decision-making processes often define our sense of whether or not a group meeting was worthwhile. Groups work better when they have shared process and outcome expectations.

Unanimity.

"It was unanimous!"–A unanimous decision is the outcome of a vote in which all members vote the same.

Consensus.

"We need to come to a consensus."—consensus (coming to a general agreement about a topic) is a process often proclaimed as an outcome.

- Critical Mass. A decision-making process in which all members of a group share their knowledge and opinions, discuss the issue, and agree to a direction that represents the maximum area of common acceptance at that moment.

  A good consensus process develops broad support for a decision. Even if not every group member can fully support the direction, the body as a whole is clearly persuaded.

- Consensus Benefits. When practiced faithfully, a consensus process often leads to high levels of: (1) agreement with group decisions, (2) commitment to group decisions, (3) satisfaction with personal participation, and (4) satisfaction with group process.

- Bait and Switch. Beware! "Consensus" has such positive associations that chairs like us are tempted to claim consensus when what actually happened was a typical group discussion resulting in a legitimate chair decision or majority vote.

- Not Unanimity. A consensus is not a unanimous vote. As an outcome, consensus defines a limited, provisional agreement on action a group can take moving forward.

Common consent.

"So ordered, without objection." Common consent is an informal, but official, group agreement. When the chair asks for objections to a proposed decision and no one responds, then the item is approved and work proceeds. Common consent is often reserved for procedural matters and involves little to no discussion.

Consent Agendas

If you want passive, disengaged group members, read previous meeting minutes at the beginning of each meeting. Then spend group meeting time discussing wording changes, typos, etc.

If not, consider a "consent agenda" as an alternative.

A consent agenda packages routine items that need official group approval, but not group discussion. Consent agenda items include meeting minutes, routine requests, notification and approval of dates and events, and anything else that is a non-controversial, "no-brainer" item. The group approves the consent agenda in a single action, without discussion, and moves on to substantive issues.

All consent agenda items go to group members prior to the meeting. If a member sees a substantive issue and wants to discuss it, the item is added to the regular agenda at their request. All typos, wording changes, and detail questions are handled outside of the meeting.

Design your meetings to capitalize on the communication advantages that come from gathering people in a group for deliberation, creativity, and decision-making. Put nothing on the agenda that can be managed outside of the meeting context.

Meeting Management Pitfalls

As chair, you need to be decisive in planning and leading a meeting. Indecision by the chair puts the purpose of the meeting and participant morale in jeopardy.

No meeting necessary.

> *Cancel routine meetings when there's no reason to meet (except that the meeting is scheduled).* "We met because we were supposed to meet" is a common, but lame, reason to bore human beings. Nothing builds group morale quite like the cancellation of an unnecessary meeting.

No referee.

> *Chair is too "nice" to interrupt, draw out, or protect.* You run the process and enforce the ground rules. No one else can. Part of your role is to cultivate healthy participation. Intense interaction is great, but you need to temper dominating members, engage quieter members, and shut down bullies.

No focus.

Tell people their roles and tasks. Meetings are not spontaneously productive and energizing. When you frame the meeting and initiate the action, people respond well. When you make it up as you go, people get discouraged or worse.

TEACHING AND TRAINING

Use public speaking principles and skills to lead people into substantial learning opportunities. People come into instructional situations with different backgrounds, learning styles, and priorities. Three elements contribute to dynamic instructional environments. People learn well in groups when they can:

Interact with ideas.

Give learners great ingredients. Quality learning begins with excellent content. A common sentiment says education is about the journey, not the destination. But substance defines the quality of the journey, not process.

Interact with the instructor.

Teach with your whole person. Your presence provides much of the richness of face-to-face instruction. You bring ideas to life personally.

Interact with participants.

Create contexts where participants can engage one another creatively and constructively. Working with peers sharpens understanding. We grasp knowledge better when explaining, questioning, and contributing ideas together.

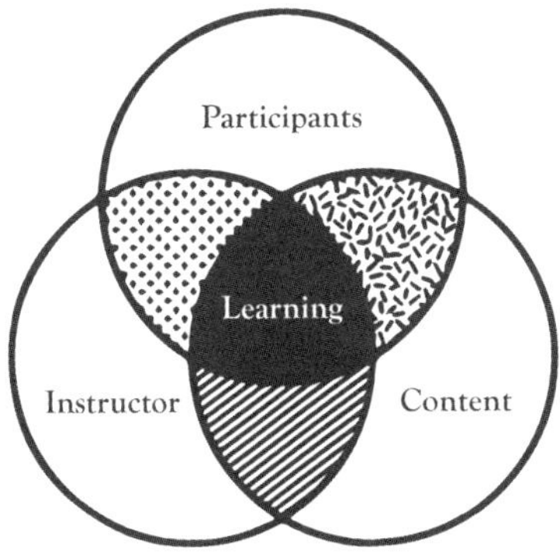

Teaching and Training Components

Rely on a set of basic communication practices to stimulate meaningful interaction. Traditional and non-traditional learners thrive in active learning environments. Interactive instruction integrates the following practices to lead participants in significant learning experiences:

Texts and lecture.

> *Bring pivotal content to each session.* Rigorous learning begins with stimulating and challenging ideas. Your first task is to arrange encounters with consequential material, which comes in many forms.

Questions.

> *Provoke thought and response through good questions.* Help people open material, gain insight, and generate questions. One good question can propel an entire session.

Discussion.

> *Get participants to think out loud together.* Good content often has an unfamiliar feel to it. Work through material in conversation with participants. It can help them process their thoughts and make important connections.

Activities.

> *Design specific tasks that highlight content and coordinate interaction.* Problems, puzzles, and projects focus attention and stimulate group participation.

What Makes Interaction Prime?

As students, we usually only look like we're listening in the classroom.

Few schools offer specific classes, let along courses of study, on listening. But in classroom contexts, most of us are trained listeners...or non-listeners, that is.

Teachers of primary-aged children are lucky. They know when their students are paying attention, and when they are, they absorb information like sponges. Five- and six-year-olds don't know how to pretend they're paying attention.

By the time we get into intermediate grades and high school, most of us have mastered the ability to give the impression that we're listening, even when our minds are worlds away. In teaching and training sessions, we often look like we're listening...but we're not.

That's one reason why, from a communication perspective, it's a high priority to put young people and adults to work actively in instructional contexts.

Activities: Define and Visualize

To use a group activity in class, clearly identify the:

1. TASK: Define the task clearly for participants.
2. DIRECTIONS: Provide the steps necessary to complete the activity.
3. TIME: Set a time limit.
4. SPOKESPERSON: Establish a reporting mechanism.

Groups do better at activities when the directions are spelled out on a visual or handout.

Prepare a Communication Lesson Plan

Follow basic lesson-planning protocols to prepare for a teaching/training sequence. These basic elements can be adapted equally well for a traditional classroom or a multi-session training context.

Why? Establish session purpose.

What's the basic reason for people to participate? State the purpose of the session by answering what one thing you want participants to be able to understand at the end of the session.

A purpose question asks, "What was the session about today?" An answer could be, "Women and men have different expectations about communication in personal relationships."

What? Develop learning objectives.

What content benchmarks do you have to hit to achieve your purpose in the session? List objectives that focus learning on specific ideas, applications, practices, etc.

For example, if someone asked, "What did you cover in class today?," an answer for a class session on gender communication might be: "'Nature and nurture' explanations for differences in how men and women communicate. Some think gender communication is mostly about our physical makeup as males and females; others think it's mostly about cultural roles—expectations about what it means 'to talk and act like a woman' and what it means to 'talk and act like a man.'"

How? Prepare a working agenda.

What components will you use to accomplish the purpose and achieve objectives for the session? Design a coherent plan with teaching and training components that will help people engage good content.

For whom? Adapt to participants.

What connections can you make between the content of the session and the lives of participants? To move people from the familiar to the unfamiliar—a reliable learning pattern—you have to find starting points within their frame of reference.

Build a Working Agenda

A working agenda should include four basic components:

Agenda item.

Create a detailed plan for each agenda item. The plan may involve one activity or a combination. Write out the questions you plan to ask, work out discussion details, list specific directions for activities, and prepare a keyword outline for lecture. If you plan to use a whiteboard or flipchart, plan it in your working agenda.

Time frame.

Allot class time for each agenda item. Review timing for the session as a whole, including a start-up activity and summary. Remember, discussions and group activities take a good deal of time.

Rationale.

Record your reasoning for each agenda item. Explain your approach to the agenda item and note the connection to learning objectives for the session.

Assessment.

Note ways to analyze an item's learning impact. Suggest how to assess each agenda item as a learning experience. Not every good element of a session will be easy to evaluate. But don't forego an activity just because you can't measure a specific outcome.

Note that working through assessment checks is important when both educational institutions and the marketplace are putting so much emphasis on measurable outcomes for teaching and training.

Instruction as Performance (Not Entertainment)

Teaching and training are performance activities. Instructors are not entertainers, but good instruction demands performance skills. As many ancient rhetoricians and educators have noted, people often need to be delighted in order to learn. (And some kinds of learning are delightful!)

So what are some differences between entertainment and instructional performance?

The most profound difference is purpose. The nature of much entertainment is to distract the mind; even most works of suspense, terror, and tragedy are designed ultimately to amuse us. Not so with instructional performance.

Performances that cause educational delight invite us into deeper waters. They make us mindful.

Control the Instructional Space

When possible, consider arranging seating to enhance interaction. Don't get trapped in the front of the room or in just one spot.

To keep participants close to you and to one another, semi-circular or U-shaped arrangements are particularly effective, even when they need to be two rows deep. Such arrangements enable you get within one seat of any participant, make it easier for people to interact, and enhance discussion.

In rooms less conducive to interaction, try to keep people together in close proximity to you and to visual aids, and move freely around the room as much as possible. By utilizing space to its fullest, you shift the focus of attention for listeners and put more people in "front row seats" during the session.

Execute the Plan

Move into public speaking performance mode to lead people through the learning experience. Your role demands an inviting, dynamic presence that encourages people to take the content seriously and participate actively.

Post an agenda.

Provide a simple agenda for students. Participants occasionally fade out and lose focus. A posted agenda helps them stay on track with progress of the session. You can also use the agenda to move participants along, especially in cases where good discussion flourishes and threatens to take over.

Set expectations immediately.

Use the first segment of the session to establish patterns for interaction. If you expect everyone to participate, get them working and interacting early.

Start with ideas.

Direct the focus of attention to content. Invest your energy to help them engage the material. As you work your plan and they interact, a number of other good dynamics are likely to emerge. Keep content at the forefront of the session.

Cultivate a good learning climate.

Prompt participation. Create a safe context for people to explore ideas publicly; provide support for people if they make a mistake or voice unpopular viewpoints. Maintain a non-defensive posture if your ideas are questioned or challenged directly, and protect others from personal attacks.

Teaching and Training Pitfalls

Everyone makes instructional mistakes because teaching and training are too complex with too many variables to ever get things completely "right." There are, however, some more pronounced problems that this chapter seeks to avoid.

Process orientation.

Don't "believe in the process." Good teaching & training does not consist in applying good instructional methodology. The important questions in life concern knowledge and wisdom—in specific fields and in general. People can learn well in many ways from many instructional modes, but a focus on process trivializes learning.

Instructor arrogance.

Don't be wise in your own eyes. Pride (not confidence) gets in the way of good instruction. Cultivate intellectual generosity toward participants and maintain a responsive, thoughtful spirit. Wisdom speaks, but not all the time!

Facilitator posture.

A qualified instructor does not "learn as much from you today as you'll learn from me." Instruction is not facilitation. Will you learn from participants? Of course! But the balance of learning should strongly favor participants.

VISUALS

Visual aids should support the spoken message. In contexts where visual aids are appropriate, they can significantly enhance (or detract from) the speech.

Enhance engagement.

Involving multiple senses helps people understand and remember a message. Sight and sound are the most prominent human senses for symbolic communication.

Illustrate complex ideas.

A good visual can replace extensive and difficult descriptions. Why give a complicated description in words when listeners could grasp it quickly with a visual?

Map the message.

Listeners follow the message better when you provide visual cues. Even a basic agenda helps the audience follow the speech more easily.

What to Support with Visuals

Select points of the speech that can be reinforced by visual aids for greater impact. Every visual should create a strong link to the spoken message.

The proposition of the speech.

Visualize the core of the message in a simple form. If you plan to use visuals at all, clarify the main point and purpose for the audience in a way that's visible and sayable.

A mental bottleneck.

Visualize a vital idea or fact that's too intricate to describe well in words. Provide a diagram, illustration, photo, or film clip to visualize, rather than disrupting the flow of the speech.

Visual conventions.

Visualize things that people find easier to think about in graphic forms. For example, visuals make sense if your message involves geography (map), anatomy (diagram), architecture (sketch), figures (charts, graphs, numbers), or fashion (photos). Visuals also enhance many comparisons.

Working priorities.

Visualize prime ideas and supporting evidence. Put audience focus on a key number, name, comparison, fact, question, or quotation.

The Most Interesting Visual

The next time you speak, remember: You are your own best visual aid!

You are the most sophisticated, animated being in the speech. Everyone else will pay attention to you when you speak, with even some slight encouragement. This is not a "dress-for-success" moment. Appearance does matter, but the point is not for you to dress as a visual aid. That's different.

Here's the point: You need to treat yourself as a visual aid as you plan and practice your speech.

Nothing you design will come close to reaching listeners the way you can through speaking presence, eye contact, and a good speaking voice. Therefore, stay centered on your performance. The message is not in visual aids, it's in you.

Make sure that visual aids, visual management, and notes all help you to fully engage listeners with the message—in sight and sound. There's at least one visual aid in every speech. Keep it in mind as you design your next one.

POWERPOINT DEMENTIA

PowerPoint templates may improve 10% to 20% of all presentations by organizing inept, extremely disorganized speakers, at a cost of detectable intellectual damage to 80%. For statistical data, the damage level approaches dementia.

~Edward Tufte[3]

[3]Tufte, Edward R. *The Cognitive Style of PowerPoint*, Cheshire, CT: Graphics Press, 2003. [Cited in Phillip G. Clampitt, *Communicating for Managerial Effectiveness*, 3rd Edition, Thousand Oaks, CA: Sage, 2005, p. 103).

Avoid PowerPoint Design Disabilities

If you speak in the working world, you're likely to speak with PowerPoint visuals. PowerPoint has become a standard for visual aids in workplaces. People assume PowerPoint is automatically effective because it's widely used, but standard uses lead to poor visual design and poor speeches.

Many speakers use visual aids as a crutch, and, because PowerPoint has features that help organize your whole speech, we're glad for any help we can get.

PowerPoint's auto-content wizard appears to be "professional grade" and offers "help." However, the auto-content wizard violates many basic visual design principles. For instance:

Bulletitis.

> *If you follow the auto-content wizard, you can end up with slide-after-slide of bullet-point lists.* Bullet lists make even the best speakers drone. We tend to believe we need to say something about every bullet...for even five bullets per slide...for all ten slides...zzzzzz.

Monitor madness.

> *Templates tend toward small print and low contrast color schemes that look good on a monitor, but not on a big screen.* Most speakers do not adapt from the way a visual looks on a monitor compared to what it will look like on a large screen before a live audience.

Detail disorder.

> *The program invites full sentence visual designs that are well suited to the written word, but cause droning in speeches.* The slides become a manuscript that is read rather than a support for listeners.

Use PowerPoint. Just ignore templates and follow good visual principles.

Visual Design Principles

Follow basic design principles that apply to multiple forms of visuals. These principles apply to computer-generated visuals, duplicated or handmade materials, and objects.

Sequence: After speech design.

A complete message drives good visual design. It's okay to make more adjustments as you prepare visuals—that's fine tuning. Just don't drive the message with visual design.

- How Many? Less is more. Use one-visual-per-minute-maximum as a rule. Too many visuals dilute impact.
- What Kind? Simply creative. Visual aids need to be well designed and easy to manage. Busy designs and complicated handling distract from the message.
- Quality? If your audience members paid a professional seminar fee ($500+), what would your visuals look like?

Purpose: For speaking performance.

The visuals will be viewed in a live, public presentation format, not up close. All design decisions need to be made in reference to the speaking venue and audience member sight lines.

- Memorable. Design the visual so you can look at listeners. The visual is for the audience, not you. You created it and cued it, so you won't need more than a glance for recall.
- Readable. Make every symbol clear and legible. Pick fonts and graphics that keep listeners' attention on message content, not visual cryptography.
- High Visibility. Always assume someone in the audience is visually impaired. Use large print, large diagrams, large images, etc.

When in doubt, make the font bigger. For PowerPoint and transparencies, all letters on an 8.5 x 11 sheet should be easy to read at a twelve foot distance without projection.

Minimum font size?

Times New Roman 40 point.

- Color Coded. Use color strategically. Color helps your audience locate what's important. You can refer to things on the visual without staring and pointing.

  A note on word visuals. Alternate colors by concept. Distinguishing ideas by color makes the visual easier to read. This applies particularly to whiteboards, flipcharts, and other hard-copy display formats. It also works well for interactive visuals in meeting and classroom contexts.

- High Contrast. Always assume someone in the audience is colorblind. Use sharp, light/dark contrast for performance visibility. What looks pleasing on a computer monitor, or up close on a poster or flipchart, is often impossible to see when presented in the speech.

Role: Support the message.

Design visuals to add value, not stand alone. The best visuals invite people to listen more carefully to what you have to say. Visual aids are not a one-to-one visual version of the speech.

- Oversimplify. When in doubt, simplify more. Limit details on diagrams, graphs, and illustrations to the essentials that relate to your speech.

Don't visualize full forms or reports, except to identity the form as a whole. Excerpt and enlarge relevant numbers or parts of a form for specific reference.

Keep full detailed data available to show to listeners after the speech if necessary.

- Limit Words. Use words as mental prompts and labels. Words in visuals are symbolic cues, not detailed prose. If you have more than one to three words per concept, you may be writing a script, not designing a visual to support a spoken message.

- Coordinate. Design for immediate listener recognition. Visuals should harmonize with your spoken words.

  Your goal is a seamless, instant connection between the audience and the message. (Obviously, this also requires well-synchronized display of visuals in performance.)

Beat Bulletitis!

Bullet lists dominate many professional presentations. "Bulletitis" occurs when a presentation is dominated by a speaker reciting bullet lists.

Symptoms.

The effects of bulletitis are relatively easy to spot.

- Droning. Bullet lists kill vocal variety. Any listener can tell when a speaker begins a bullet list without even seeing the slide. Bullets suck the life out of your speaking voice.

- Mindless Obedience. Bullet lists coerce recitation. Speakers can't skip a single bullet. The only way to get through the list is to read faster, every word.

- Comatose Listeners. Bullet lists slay listener interest. People try, but fail. The droning and the number of bullets render the audience unconscious. They can hardly hear a thing and remember even less.

Treatment.

Most bullet lists are one or two steps from becoming good visuals. If you have a bullet list, convert it to a good visual.

- Frame a Question. Invite listeners into the material. The question can prompt an example, case study, or scenario that leads into the material.
- Create a Diagram. Present a diagram of the points or material.
- Visualize One Idea. Divide the bullet list into separate slides.

Multimedia: Video and Audio

In longer presentations, a film or audio clip may provide excellent support for a speech. Keep audience standards in mind concerning appropriate images and decent language.

Shock value is an oxymoron for grown-ups.

Advance preparation.

- Select a Brief Clip. Don't let a recording dominate your live message. Only use what has a direct, concise connection.
- Test Projection and Sound. Make sure that the clip(s) will play on the available equipment and set sound levels.
- Cue Clips. In a formal presentation, clips should be carefully cued. Drop the clip if you can't use it without a long pause or disruption.

Performance.

- Practice Tight Transitions. The crucial connection is between the clip and the speech. Give just enough context for listeners to connect the two items.
- Execute the Speech in Sync. Keep the focus on message content, not visual process. If you have any trouble, drop the clip and move on.

Boards and Flipcharts

"Finished" posters and display boards can be impressive in formal speeches. Flipcharts and whiteboards are particularly good for posting an agenda and for interactive applications.

Advance preparation.

- Create Borders. Start posters, display boards, and flipcharts with a border around the edge for a finished, professional look.
- Alternate Colors. In word visuals, distinguish one idea from another with contrasting colors.
- Hide Notes. Consider placing at-a-glance note prompts in the margins of posters, display boards, and flipcharts. They can be particularly helpful for inexperienced speakers doing long presentations.

Performance.

- Secure for Display. Bring tape, binder clips, and push pins/thumb tacks to attach visual aids securely to an easel, board, or wall. Don't get distracted by the visual during the speech.
- Presentation Position. Set up the visual aid opposite your dominant hand. If you need to make adjustments, turn to the visual, work with your dominant hand, and return to your speaking position. Positioning is especially important if you write on a whiteboard or flipchart interactively.

Take Rare Visual Exceptions

What are some exceptions to the rule on limiting words in good visuals?

Sentences.

A few statements are worth full sentence form. Examples: the proposition of the speech, a key piece of evidence, a mission statement, or a provocative statement at the introduction or conclusion of the speech.

Questions.

A simple question can serve a triple purpose. It can enhance attention, illustrate a main idea, and guide the speech. You can keep the question posted as you work through the issue.

Quotations.

Rather than trying to memorize a quotation or read it from notes, make a visual. Sparse use of quotations gives good support and mental momentum for the message.

Design and delivery.

- Frame One Statement Per Visual. Keep the statement, question, or quotation simple.
- Use Maximum Print Size. Visibility is crucial. Don't resort to small type to make it fit.
- Read Aloud. Point listeners to the full statement and read it verbatim. This is a major exception. No other visuals should be read out loud word-for-word!

Plan to Present with Visuals

Visuals last.

Prepare visuals as the last stage of speech design. The whole message should be complete in full preliminary form including content, structure, and initial speaking notes.

Prior to performance.

Speakers make many avoidable errors in setting up their visuals. The best visual aids in the world will fail if you are not prepared in advance to use them.

- Test All Audio/Visual Equipment. Arrive in enough time to check out every piece of equipment that you intend to use. Check all electronics, technology, etc., and the stability of your flipcharts/easel.

- Place Visuals Strategically. Based on your position, locate the poster, TV monitor, flipcharts, and other equipment where you can operate or refer to them with minimal distraction for you and the audience.

- Check for Audience View. Confirm that your listeners will be able to see all your visuals clearly. Physically move to the different places people will be seated and check the view from their perspective.

Avoid visual magnetism.

Visual aids tempt speakers to speak to the visuals instead of the audience. Refuse their seduction!

- Work Forward of Your Visuals. They will tempt you to take refuge from the audience as far back in the room as possible. Use color in visual design so you can make references without pointing or needing a laser pointer.

- Don't Read Visual Aids Verbatim. The audience can read. The visual should serve as a support; it should not present the entire message.

- Move Away From Equipment. Limit your contact with your visuals and visual equipment to what is necessary for use or adjustment. Maintain distance from screens, monitors, keyboards, etc. as much as possible.

Review and practice.

Practice is essential to effective visual management. Complete your visuals prior to practice. Unfamiliarity breeds visual magnetism in performance.

Speak to Listeners, Not to Visuals

Stop speaking to the visual aids! Audiences notice.

Working professionals and students all tell the same, sad story. When asked what speakers do that gets in the way of their message, people say, "They stand up front, change from one slide to the next, stare at the screen, and read every slide word-for-word. They ignore the audience."

Follow up question: "Are these people beginners?" Reply: "No. That's the boss;" or, "No, all the vice-presidents do the same thing;" or worse, "That's what they expect us all to do. I might get a bad performance appraisal if I do something different than they do."

Handouts Are Not Visuals: Guidelines for Proper Use

Your message may call for an audience handout. Many good speeches do benefit from a handout and some demand one. Handouts are not visual aids–they send listeners into their own little worlds. Do not pass them out while you are presenting a speech.

The trick is when and how to incorporate handouts with the speech.

When speakers distribute a handout, they lose audience attention twice: Once as the handout is distributed and again as people read it.

Options for formal presentations.

- Distribute in Advance. Give listeners a handout before the speech. People can read the material, and then you can refer to it in the message. If your message is based on complex data or an extensive document, provide a simplified version as a speech handout.
- Mention in the Speech and Distribute Afterwards. Tell listeners to expect a handout after the speech and give highlights during the speech. Distribute copies when you conclude.
- Offer at the Conclusion. Make no reference to a handout, but provide it immediately after the speech is over.

In many professional contexts, handouts provide important printed information and enhance speaker credibility. Distribute detailed versions of forms, reports, diagrams, and other documents that you discussed or visualized only in a simplified form.

Options for informal and interactive contexts.

Handouts often work well, but plan distribution with care. Keep the focus on the spoken message and use the handout for the value-added purpose it should serve. Avoid handout hubbub to the greatest degree possible.

Visual Pitfalls

Visual crutches.

Prepare the speech so you could give it without visuals. Visuals can truly aid the speech, but you should always be able to perform the message well without them.

Visual manuscript.

Keep your eyes on your listeners, not the visual aids. Reading visuals has the same deadening effect as a manuscript or note dependence.

Techno-overkill.

Don't let the technology dominate the message. Sophisticated production, graphics, or animations does not mean visuals will support or contribute to the message.